HEALTHY SKIN AND COAT

Dunbar Gram, DVM

Photography: Joan Balzarini, Isabelle Francais, Dunbar Gram, DVM, Robert Pearcy, Dr. Jon Plant

Distributed in the UNITED STATES to the Pet Trade by T.F.H. Publications, Inc., 1 TFH Plaza, Neptune City, NJ 07753; on the Internet at www.tfh.com; in CANADA by Rolf C. Hagen Inc., 3225 Sartelon St., Montreal, Quebec H4R 1E8; Pet Trade by H & L Pet Supplies Inc., 27 Kingston Crescent, Kitchener, Ontario N2B 2T6; in ENGLAND by T.F.H. Publications, PO Box 74, Havant PO9 5TT; in AUSTRALIA AND THE SOUTH PACIFIC by T.F.H. (Australia), Pty. Ltd., Box 149, Brookvale 2100 N.S.W., Australia; in NEW ZEALAND by Brooklands Aquarium Ltd., 5 McGiven Drive, New Plymouth, RD1 New Zealand; in SOUTH AFRICA by Rolf C. Hagen S.A. (PTY.) LTD., P.O. Box 201199, Durban North 4016, South Africa; in JAPAN by T.F.H. Publications. Published by T.F.H. Publications, Inc.
MANUFACTURED IN THE
UNITED STATES OF AMERICA
BY T.F.H. PUBLICATIONS, INC.

Your cat's overall health is reflected in the appearance of his skin and coat.

INTRODUCTION

This publication provides general information regarding the skin and various skin conditions. It is by no means complete or a substitute for veterinary care. The cause of a pet's skin problem is often difficult, if not impossible, to determine without performing diagnostic tests and/or monitoring response to treatment. In some patients, more than one disease may be causing a problem.

Infections and other diseases may come and go with therapy or sometimes due to other factors. Additionally, a normal test result at one time does not mean that the disease will not be, or was not, present at a different time. Reevaluations by a veterinarian may reveal different symptoms of the same disease or the presence of a new disease. It is important to differentiate these two possibilities from the third possibility, which is treatment failure.

With many chronic and incurable diseases, several different treatment options may be attempted before finding one that works for each individual. If symptoms are due to an unusual, chronic, or difficult-to-manage disease, your veterinarian may recommend that your pet see a veterinary dermatologist. A board-certified veterinary dermatologist has received a minimum of two to three years of additional training after completing veterinary school, and successfully completed examinations administered by the American College of Veterinary Dermatology. At the time of this publication there were approximately 104 of these board-certified specialists in the world. Many of these vetrinarians work at a veterinary school, but an increasing number can be found in private practice.

Consultation with your veterinarian will allow you to secure a professional diagnosis of your cat's skin ailments, and establish a protocol of proper care.

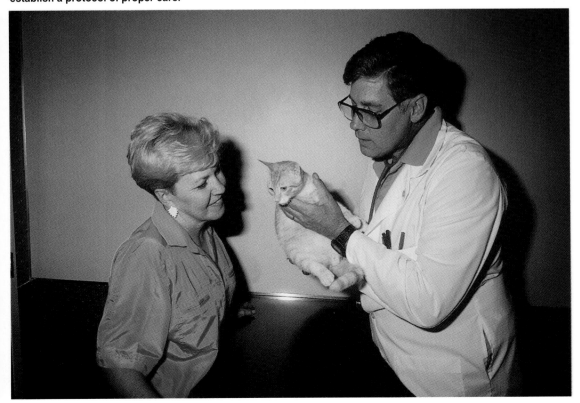

ABOUT THE SKIN

The skin is the largest organ in the body. It performs a variety of functions to protect and to sustain life. These functions include enclosing the body while allowing movement, and protecting it from outside environmental influences. The skin needs to be flexible enough to not restrict activity, yet tough enough to protect your pet from such minor trauma as scratches and bumps, as well as irritants and toxins that might otherwise get into the body.

In this respect, the skin is much like a wet suit used in many water sports. Protection in the form of pigment deposition in the deeper layers helps to minimize damage by solar radiation.

Temperature regulation is another important function performed in this part of the body. This is controlled through sweat glands and the blood supply. Sweat glands act primarily through evaporation, although these glands are limited in number and distribution in most pets. The blood vessels in the skin will dilate, or widen, to allow heat brought by the blood from the core of the body to escape from the surface. Conversely, constriction, or narrowing of the vessels helps to conserve heat.

Hair is produced in the skin and aids in thermoregulation and physical protection as

Good grooming helps to prevent tangles and mats in your cat's coat, which can lead to more serious skin problems.

well as appearance. Through the use of tiny muscles in the skin, the hair shafts can stand erect to allow heat to escape from the surface of the skin, or these shafts may lie down, creating a thin, insulating layer of air against the body. The hair coat provides another layer of protection against trauma. Hairs are deceptively tough, as demonstrated by how quickly the blades of scissors or a knife can become dull when cutting hair. Excessive chewing of hair by itching animals may actually wear down the teeth.

An animal's appearance with respect to the hair coat is important in socialization, mating, and survival. When your pets' ancestors lived in the wild, the color and pattern of the hair coat acted as camouflage to protect them from predators as well as to allow them to hunt prey. The same muscles that help regulate the body temperature can make the hairs stand erect during confrontation, which is believed to act as non-verbal communication and to make the animal appear larger.

The skin also is an integral part of the immune system, protecting the body from infection by bacteria, fungi, and viruses as well as helping to prevent the development of tumors. In addition to acting as a physical barrier, there are several types of cells that live in the layers of the skin that act to swallow many of these potentially harmful organisms. Some of these cells are believed to help prevent the formation of some skin tumors by eliminating abnormal cells. The blood vessels also help by bringing other components of the immune system to the skin when needed. Sebum and sweat produced by glands in the skin also contain many ingredients such as immunoglobulins to help fight off infection. The skin provides nerves for sensory perception. These nerves help the individual perceive heat,

The cat's coat was originally intended as camouflage against natural predators. This Bengal blends right in with the scenery.

cold, pain, itch, and pressure, as well as a sense of touch, all of which are necessary for interaction with the environment and survival.

There are different types of glands found in the skin. In addition to the previously mentioned properties of thermoregulation and immune protection, other functions of the glands, such as excreting waste material to a certain extent and producing and secreting a variety of substances, are performed here. For example, the sebaceous glands produce sebum, which acts to help keep the skin soft and well-hydrated in addition to its immune defense contribution.

Such substances as fat, protein, and electrolytes are stored in the skin. These materials can be easily retrieved when needed by the rest of the body. This organ is also an important source of vitamin D, which is necessary for the regulation of calcium.

Because of the many functions of the skin and its constantly changing, or dynamic, nature, the skin is a window into the overall health status of the animal. Abnormalities in any part of the process will be revealed in the end result. For example, poor nutrition brought about by poor quality pet foods or an incompletely formulated diet may manifest itself as a dull, brittle, or dry hair coat, poor hair coloration, lusterless skin, dry scaling, or any combination of these characteristics. As the skin is a storage organ, an abnormal appearance or texture may indicate a deficiency of one or several of the nutrients needed by the body.

The level of hydration may also be assessed by the skin. While one of its functions is to protect the body from exposure to foreign material or harmful substances, is very important in preventing the loss of life-sustaining fluid. A pet suffering from dehydration may have skin that feels tacky and does not slide easily over the underlying muscles. Dull or flaky skin may indicate an imbalance of vitamins or essential fatty acids.

Many deficiencies produce similar changes in the skin, so it is very important to know which component is causing the problem. Arbitrary supplementation with nutritional or vitamin supplements may actually cause more harm by creating excessive quantities and/or imbalances of nutrients. The harm may not only be to the skin but to other organs in the body as well. It is best to have your pet examined by a

veterinarian before adding anything to the diet. Generally, a good quality, balanced commercial pet food is sufficient for the well-being of the animal. Animals with abnormalities in nutritional requirements or in absorption capabilities may need specific nutritional assistance.

Hair growth is an ongoing process, so bodily changes can be mirrored in this structure also. The hair growth cycle is affected by day length, temperature, hormones, nutrition, genetics, illness, and other less defined influences. Changes to any of these factors can alter the cycle and appearance of the hair coat. Many different alterations can produce similar changes in the hair so again, it is important to ascertain the specific problem. As the skin and hair are constantly changing and growing, it is easy to see how poor quality or deficiency of

Your feline friend will reap the benefits of proper nutrition: healthy skin and coat, bright eyes, plenty of energy, and all-around good health. Photo courtesy of Nutro.

The naturally thin coat of the Cornish Rex offers a rare glimpse into the design of cat skin that cannot be seen in more hirsute breeds.

the necessary building blocks, (i.e. dietary nutrients) can produce an abnormal appearance and impair the many functions of these structures.

Additionally, when the hair coat is compromised for whatever reason—for example, trauma from rubbing or scratching, or from hormonal changes, the skin loses some of its protection and opportunistic infections can develop.

Knowing the structure of the skin helps in understanding the changes in appearance that may be seen. Basically the skin forms in layers, consisting of the epidermis—the outermost layer, the dermis—the supporting layer, and the panniculus, which is essentially the subcutaneous fat.

The epidermis is subdivided into layers within itself. These layers are not separate entities but are different stages of a continual cycle. The basal cell layer, or bottom layer of the epidermis, is where the cells are born. These cells "mature," or keratinize, proceeding to form the outermost layer, the stratum corneum, or horny cell layer. (One way to think of this process is to compare it to the mass production of cookies. The basal cells are like spoonfuls of cookie dough that flatten and harden as they bake, moving on a conveyer belt through the oven, and resulting in the final product that may be stacked more tightly and into a smaller space. The outermost cells normally slough off into the environment).

In the normal animal, the speed and degree to which this happens is so subtle that these dead cells are barely noticeable. In certain types of abnormal skin (such as seborrhea), the cycle is accelerated, producing larger sheets of dead cells, seen as

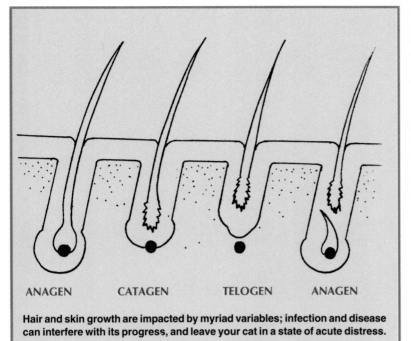

ANAGEN   CATAGEN   TELOGEN   ANAGEN

Hair and skin growth are impacted by myriad variables; infection and disease can interfere with its progress, and leave your cat in a state of acute distress.

of the hair cycle. This prevents bare patches and subsequent loss of protection. Therefore when the skin can be seen due to the lack of hair in an area that previously had hair, this indicates a disruption in the cycle, and warrants investigation of the many influencing factors. For example, hairs in the telogen, or resting, phase, remain in the follicle but may be more easily lost by the nature of their attachment in comparison to those in the anagen, or growing, phase. Therefore if more hairs in one area are in the telogen phase, this area is more likely to have hair loss and a subsequent bald patch.

This situation can occur by shortening the anagen phase as occurs in illness. The body shifts its energy and nutrients toward fighting the illness and away from growth. The appearance of the hair itself may be changed by any number of influences (such as illness or nutritional deficiencies) that may be involved in any number of the steps required for hair formation. The hair bulb, which is where the hair begins, is influenced by a variety of hormones, including glucocorticosteroids and sex hormones. Any number of imbalances with these substances may lead to alterations in the hair cycle. However, it is important to note that neutering your pet will not create a problem in the hair coat.

The skin is a constantly changing, complex organ that may be affected by numerous external and internal

white flakes. This change may be due to inflammation, infection, hormonal changes, or a dysfunction of the basal cells. Also, there is a significant amount of fluid in all layers of the skin, helping to hold the outermost cells together. With dry skin, such as can occur in the winter with dry heat indoors, more fluid is lost by evaporation, leading to more cells falling off the surface or flaking.

The stratum corneum (horny cell layer) can be likened to a brick wall. The bricks are held together by mortar, a paste-like material with a significant portion that is water. Without the water, the mortar is just powder that cannot hold the bricks together. The "mortar" in the skin also contains a large amount of balanced fatty acids. Alteration of the balance, or amount, of fatty

acids may lead to disruption of the "brick" wall. This is just one example of the differences in appearance that indicate a problem in the animal's health.

The hair can also demonstrate changes that indicate problems in the body. The hair grows in a cycle consisting essentially of three parts. The anagen phase is the active growing phase of the cycle. This phase is followed by the catagen phase, which is the time the hair follicle returns to its original form after growth. The last phase is the telogen phase, which is the resting period of the hair follicle. These phases vary in length due to genetic variances between breeds. In the normal animal, the individual hair follicles differ slightly from one another with respect to the particular part

This cat was diagnosed with squamous cell carcinoma, which resulted in hair loss and severe trauma to the nose.

influences. The skin and hair coat can indicate underlying or impending disorders. Its many duties and functions are necessary for the survival of your pet. A well-balanced diet and maintenance care, such as grooming and bathing, will allow skin its optimal protection capacity, and provide your pet with a healthy, happy life.

A closer view of the cat's skin cancer points out the destructive nature of this condition.

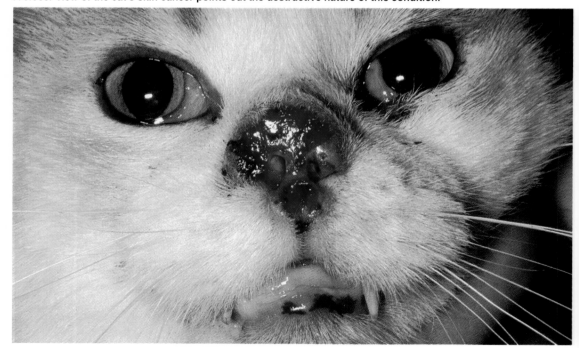

GROOMING AND BATHING FOR GOOD HEALTH

The grooming and bathing needs for cats are different than those for dogs. In general, cats are meticulous about grooming themselves, and pets without a skin problem may only require periodic brushing and never need a bath. Overweight cats may have difficulty reaching and cleaning certain areas of their body and require additional attention.

Outdoor pets are more likely to come into contact with various substances that are best removed by bathing rather than by the cats themselves. Cats with certain skin problems may often benefit from baths as often as once a week, and the use of a special shampoo or other topical application. While some cats may actually seem to enjoy a bath, many may not be appreciative and require extra patience and effort. Consultation with your vet or a veterinary dermatologist may be necessary to determine which medical decisions affect your pet's bathing needs.

Under special circumstances where the condition of the coat is beyond routine grooming and bathing, or it is not practical for a pet owner to perform these procedures, a groomer can be your pet's best friend. Professional groomers have undertaken the "hair raising" task of providing cosmetic care of pets, dealing with the pet owner's expectations, working with sometimes

uncooperative animals, as well as being able to address some minor skin or ear problems before they get out

of control. They can also be a great asset in providing the proper skin care for a patient suffering from various

Bathing helps to rid the cat of the skin's impurities, and is oftentimes an essential step in calming skin disorders.

dermatological problems. Pet owners should become acquainted with a potential groomer in much the same way as their veterinarian, family doctor or pediatrician. Young cats should become accustomed to being brushed. Please keep in mind that grooming can be very difficult work, and a great deal of time may be spent trying to gently take care of mats and other problems. Although most pet owners are appreciative of this, not all pets understand that you and their groomer are working to improve their health and appearance.

Regular grooming involves more than brushing, bathing, and drying. Conditioning, combing, dematting, nail trimming, ear cleaning and occasionally anal sac evacuation are all part of the task. Brushing is probably the most important activity that an owner can perform. The skin of the cat is thinner and more fragile than that of a dog.

Brushing should be performed with care, and some types of grooming tools used in dogs are not appropriate for cats. An additional factor to consider with cats is their sometimes uncooperative nature, and the added potential for the pet caretaker to be scratched or bitten.

Cat bites or scratches can become severely infected. With most bites, a visit to your own physician is advisable to decrease the potential for a serious problem. Many cats look forward to brushing as a daily or weekly ritual. The length of the hair coat leads to vastly different grooming requirements. Frequent brushing will help to evenly distribute the coat's natural oils, decrease shedding into the environment, and provide the opportunity to closely evaluate the condition of your pet's skin, hair, ears, nails, and feet. It is also a good opportunity to examine the teeth if routine dental care is not part of the pet's regimen. Many times human members of the household report that the pet's skin has a bad odor. In reality, a bad odor may be due to the condition of the teeth or gums.

There are many different types of brushes, some best suited for particular types of hair coats. A natural bristle brush is often appropriate for cats with short hair. It may first be used backwards against the direction of growth of hair and then in the direction of growth. "Wiping" the coat afterward (in the direction of the hair growth) with a piece of chamois or velvet will help give the coat a more "groomed and polished" appearance.

Cats with longer hair will require the use of a slicker brush. Slicker brushes are available in a variety of sizes and styles. They usually consist of a rectangular head with fine, close metal bristles that may be bent or somewhat resemble a "bed of nails." The most gentle type available should be the type used with cats. To use it, the hair is lifted and parted; then gently brushed out from the skin in layers in somewhat similar fashion to using a rake in small strokes to move a pile of leaves. Mats or knotted areas may be pulled apart ever so gently with the use of fingers.

Shampoos and lotions can dry out skin and coat, which can lead to serious health problems. Formulations that include the soothing and anti-bacterial, anti-fungal agent tea-tree oil are gentle on skin and coat. They're gentle enough to use everyday, yet strong enough to control itching and odors, and to relieve dry skin problems. Photo courtesy of Bonza Pet Care Products.

It is very important to be gentle and not damage or hurt the skin. An initial grooming and brushing by a professional groomer is a great way to get started as they may also be able to help by selecting the correct type of brush to use and provide instruction on how to use it. Periodic visits to the groomer will also help ensure that nothing is overlooked.

Frequent brushing helps prevent mats, but they may still occur. Mats should be handled very cautiously. Often they can be worked out with the use of fingers to pull the mat into smaller pieces and eventually individual hairs. A similar technique may be used with burrs or grass awns. If attempted mat removal causes too much discomfort, it is probably better to clip out the mat. Electric clippers are better than scissors because scissors may cut the underlying skin. Removal of mats may reveal a problem that actually caused the formation of mats or a problem that was the result of mat formation. Medical attention may be necessary in some severe cases.

Selecting the proper shampoo for your pet can be a daunting task. An all-natural shampoo is not necessarily a better shampoo. Individual preference, your pet's type and condition of coat, and the presence of skin problems will dictate which shampoo is best for each bath. In many cases, a healthy cat may never need bathing. However, a mild shampoo may occasionally be required. The coat should be thoroughly rinsed afterward. A conditioner may then be helpful with some types of hair coats. In certain situations, a medicated shampoo may be necessary.

The type of medicated shampoo used depends on the type of skin problem that is present. Some shampoos are best used to help control skin infections, while others are better at controlling specific conditions, such as seborrhea. Others have different indications and properties. Your pet's shampoo requirements will likely change over time. A shampoo that is appropriate when one dermatological condition is present may not be appropriate at another time.

It is important to read the shampoo bottle label for bathing instructions, and to ensure that the product is designed specifically for cats.

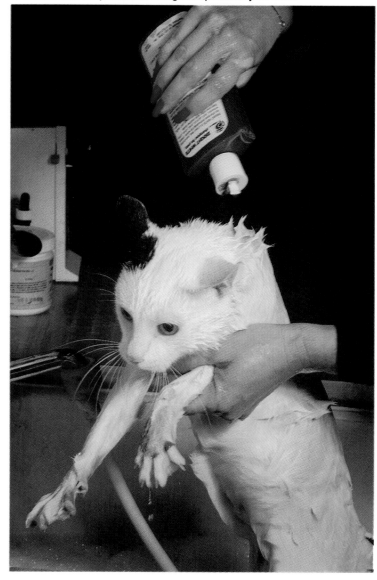

Conditioners are now available to address dry skin complaints and add lustrous sheen to the cat's coat.

It is also important to note that shampoos are seldom a "cure all." When the correct shampoo is utilized in an appropriate manner, it can be of significant benefit. However, in many situations, shampoo therapy alone may not be enough.

Medicated shampoos may be utilized as part of a long-term maintenance program for a pet diagnosed with a certain dermatological condition. Medicated shampoos may also be used as a means to control a problem in the short-term or while waiting for the results of medical tests. Not all dermatological conditions respond well to shampoo therapy.

With chronic conditions, it is important to try to have a confirmed diagnosis of what is causing the skin problem. Various diagnostic tests may be recommended by your veterinarian or veterinary dermatologist as part of a plan to identify and treat your pet's skin condition. Without a confirmed diagnosis, it may not be possible to determine which shampoo is best. A shampoo may not work well because it may not address the particular disease affecting your pet. In some cases, shampoo and even water alone may cause greater irritation. It is possible that the best shampoo available may not be appropriate or adequate. Additional types of therapy (pills or injections) may be necessary.

Antimicrobial shampoos help control infections. They may be used as a sole treatment in mild infections, or to prevent the infections from coming back. When used properly, they may also help prevent the spread of such diseases as ringworm. With more complex infections, antimocrobial shampoo may also be used in conjunction with oral medications (pills or liquids) to help speed the recovery process, and more quickly improve quality of the hair and skin infections. Remember that cats are sensitive to some topical medications. Please make sure that a particular product's label states that it is specifically for use on cats. Four of the more common types of ingredients in antimicrobial shampoos include chlorhexidine, ethyl lactate, benzoyl peroxide, and iodine. Iodine is actually seldom used anymore because of its potential to stain, irritate, and cause allergic reactions. Chlorhexidine and ethyl lactate are usually well tolerated and effective. Benzoyl peroxide may be found alone or in combination with other ingredients. It is quite effective and helps decrease "greasiness" but can be irritating. All of the above ingredients have activity against bacteria, but only the chlorhexidine and iodine have properties that fight fungi (and yeast). Recently, new shampoos have been released that have better activity against fungal organisms. However, topical therapy alone is not always enough for some of these organisms.

Another new development in the field of topical therapy includes the use of "leave-on conditioners" that are applied to the wet skin and hair coat after shampooing. They may contain different antimicrobial or soothing ingredients. These products are not rinsed off after application.

Antiseborrheic shampoos may be used to help control conditions ranging from dry scales or flakes (dandruff) to a greasy and oily hair coat. Shampoo therapy is an indispensable part of therapy for a pet suffering from primary seborrhea. It is also

The epidermis, dermis and panniculus represent the major building blocks of the skin. Layer upon layer, they produce the skin and coat, and inevitably create the feline companion you call your cat. Lacking a full coat, these two Devon Rex cats are more susceptible to certain skin conditions and injury.

an extremely important factor in controlling secondary seborrhea until the underlying reason can be diagnosed and treated. Fortunately, cats seldom get primary seborrhea. Antiseborrheic shampoos help decrease scale or dandruff by either decreasing scale formation or speeding its removal from the skin and coat. Examples of ingredients that can help with this problem include sulfur and salicylic acid. Benzoyl peroxide helps decrease greasiness and speed removal of scales and flakes but can also be drying or irritating. Often two or more of these ingredients may be combined into one product to improve efficacy.

The use of generic products should be avoided because quality control and the correct mixture of ingredients is necessary to obtain the best results. Tar shampoos are virtually never used in cats because of their potential problems. Often, antiseborrheic shampoos do not provide what we would expect in lathering action. However, this does not mean that they are not effective in their intended purpose. If your cat is patient enough, it may be beneficial to bathe with a general cleaning shampoo before using any medicated shampoo.

Flea shampoos are helpful in the short term to control fleas; they do not provide long-lasting protection. The adult fleas seen on a pet actually account for approximately ten percent or less of the total flea population. Significant numbers of eggs, larvae, and pre-adult fleas remain in the environment. There are much more effective means of dealing with and preventing a flea problem. Antiparasitic shampoos and dips that are well tolerated by dogs may be unsafe in cats. Always make sure that the products you use specifically state that they may be used on cats.

Shampoos can also be used to help decrease itching. They work in two ways: They may treat diseases such as conditions that those contribute to itching, or they may be soothing and help reduce itching itself. For small, localized areas, sprays, lotions, and creams are appropriate. For larger areas, shampoos may be necessary. Colloidal oatmeal can be

Grooming is relaxing and soothing to your cat, and allows the owner to inspect the cat for signs of potential skin problems.

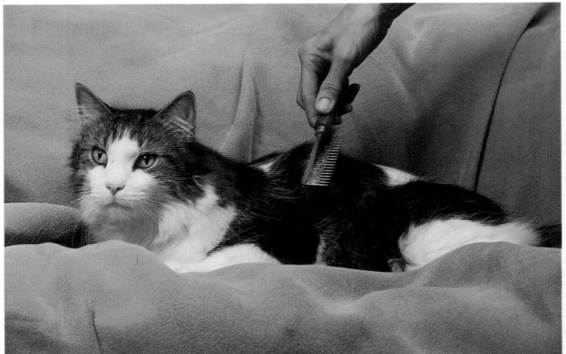

found in virtually all forms of topical therapy. In some cases, it is very beneficial, but its length of action is usually less than two days.

Topical antihistamines may be found alone or in combination with other ingredients. They have not been shown to have a beneficial effect, and with prolonged use they may result in a contact reaction. Because of this and the additional cost associated with products containing antihistamines, veterinary dermatologists seldom recommend them. Topical anesthetics may offer a very short duration of effect, and in some cases may cause a contact reaction. Other topical medications may provide very short-term relief but are seldom appropriate for

long-term control of itching.

Topical steroids are probably the most useful topical medications. However, they are not without risks. If used excessively, they can cause localized and systemic side effects. Some topical steroid medications also contain other ingredients, such as alcohol, that can irritate the skin. As with all topical medications, it is important to check the label and ask your vet if the product is safe to use on cats.

In some animals, the application of any substance, including water, can result in deterioration of the symptoms. Your pet's skin condition and shampoo needs will likely change with time and response to therapy. The use of topical medications in

more localized areas can also be very beneficial and may reduce or eliminate the need for other forms of treatment. Inappropriate use of medications can worsen a skin problem and delay the initiation of appropriate therapy.

Remember, cats are particularly sensitive to various substances and can have adverse reactions to substances that are considered safe for dogs. Read labels carefully to make sure the product is intended for use on cats. Your veterinarian or veterinary dermatologist can also recommend topical medications that are both safe and designed to improve the quality of your cat's skin and coat.

Always make sure that shampoo labels clearly state that the product is intended for use on cats.

Carefully inspect your cat's skin, coat—*and ears*—for signs of potential infection.

FIGHTING FLEAS, TICKS, AND OTHER PARASITES

FLEAS

The most common parasite to cause skin problems is the flea. In many cases, fleas complicate the task of control, it can be difficult to determine the true severity of the disease. The clinical signs of other parasitic infestations, allergies, and even some life- identifying and treating your pet's skin problem. If flea control is not effective in controlling a skin problem, or if it is an unusual problem,

Excessive scratching can be unbearable for your cat, and may also signal the presence of some form of infection.

identifying other causes of skin disease. Often, a pet's symptoms may be due to a combination of fleas and other factors. Without adequate flea threatening diseases, can be similar to symptoms linked to flea-associated dermatitis. If fleas are present, eliminating them is an important step in other possible causes should be considered.

Many people are under the false impression that if fleas or flea bites do not affect

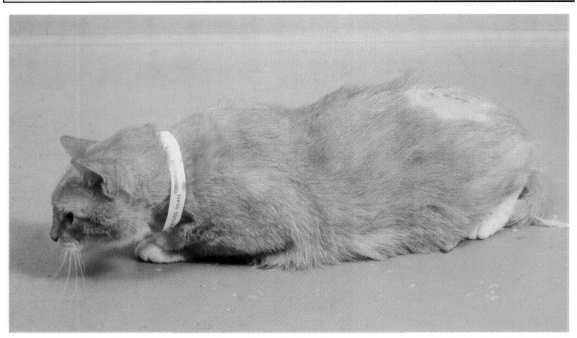

The cat pictured here shows symptoms of allergy dermatitis; the obvious symptoms are a lack of hair on the backside, and the presence of sores throughout the body.

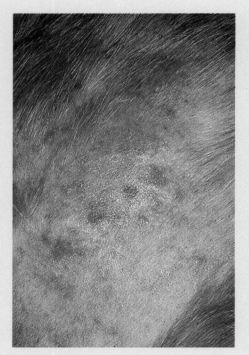

A close-up view of the sores that often accompany dermatitis.

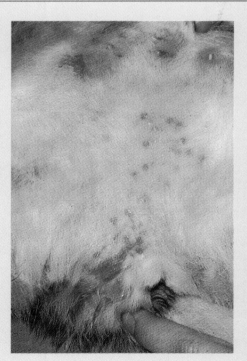

Close-up of the stomach region where eisinophilic plaque had infiltrated the skin.

humans, then fleas are not a problem for their pet. Most fleas prefer dogs and cats to humans. Mild to moderate flea infestations may not actually result in a problem for humans in the house, but a relatively few number of fleas can cause a significant problem for animals. Cats can be such efficient groomers and flea removers that they may remove fleas from their hair coat before they are detected by their owners.

Devices called "flea traps" are extremely useful in illustrating the presence of fleas in the indoors, and in emphasizing the need for environmental control of fleas. Unfortunately, they are not effective as a sole means of eliminating fleas in the house. Consultation with a vet concerning potential toxicities and effectiveness is strongly recommended when implementing any flea control program. Flea control can be an extremely frustrating process, but success can be achieved with an organized approach to the problem.

Some basic information concerning fleas is useful in addressing the solution. The cat flea is by far the most common flea to infest both dogs and cats in the US. While other types of fleas may occur, treatment using the biology of the cat flea will generally treat most other types. Flea eggs are white and quite small, approximately 0.5 millimeters in length. Depending on temperature and humidity, these eggs can hatch from one to ten days after being deposited by the female. While the eggs are deposited on the pet, they do not stick to the body or hair

and quickly fall off into the immediate environment.

The larvae that hatch are between 2 to 5 millimeters in length and are worm-like organisms that feed on organic debris and flea feces. They avoid light and move deep into the carpet or under grass, leaves, or soil. Larvae are very sensitive to heat and drying out, or desiccation. This sensitivity, in addition to the nutritional requirement of adult flea feces, allows the larvae to thrive only in selected areas where the pet spends much of its time. These areas include shaded moist ground outdoors and the carpet or spaces in hardwood floors indoors.

Once the larvae are completely developed, they produce a cocoon in which they mature into adult fleas. Prior to emerging from this cocoon, the adults are in their most protected state. Inside, they are resistant to drying out and to insecticides. This stage can protect the adult for up to 140 days until the right stimulus occurs to induce the emergence from the cocoon. This can be physical pressure, heat, or carbon dioxide. (Vibration has been considered to be a factor as well but has not been proven by research.) The variable length of this stage helps ensure survival when conditions are right. It is the shortest under ideal conditions, such as those found in the home, and can lead to a life cycle of only two to four weeks.

After emergence, the adult flea is attracted to light and avoids the deeper carpet or vegetation in an effort to be closer to a passing animal.

Contrary to previous thought, the flea spends the majority of its time on the pet. They generally live for only a matter of days when removed from your pet's body. Fleas are attracted to the pet by body heat, carbon dioxide, and movement; they move primarily only when stimulated.

The female flea requires blood as a first meal, which is obtained by biting your pet, in order to begin producing eggs. These females are capable of producing several thousands of eggs in their lifetime. To make this many eggs, a large amount of food, (i.e. blood), is necessary. This is evident by the life-threatening anemia that may occur in animals with a heavy infestation of fleas. Male fleas feed as well but to a lesser degree. While feeding, fleas excrete digested blood that appears as pepper-like material known as flea dirt on the pet. Occasionally this is mistakenly identified as eggs. Flea dirt will color water red, indicating the original source as blood.

With this basic knowledge of fleas, treatment for fleas can be adjusted to provide the most complete control. While fleas do spend most of their time on the pet, control is still essentially a three-pronged attack, targeting the yard, the house, and the pet. It is important to remember that wild and stray animals can be a continuing source of fleas in the yard, crawl spaces and attics. Also, bearing in mind the adaptive length of the cocoon phase of the flea's life cycle, a sudden increase in fleas in the home after a vacation may not be from the boarding facility where your pet was staying, but the result of stimulation of the emerging adult flea population upon your return.

This is an exciting time for controlling fleas, as there are many new advances in products based on the discovery of different aspects of the flea's biology. Killing the biting and breeding adult flea is certainly one important part of the process; equally important is avoiding the more numerous immature fleas from becoming adult fleas.

This second part of this process is performed with a group of compounds called "insect growth regulators," which block the development of the immature stages. More recently, agents have been developed to damage or kill eggs and larvae. In the yard, a spray to kill adult fleas can be used every two weeks for

several treatments during the prime flea season to eliminate the emerging adult fleas. The addition of an insect growth regulator enhances the effectiveness and provides greater long-term control. Many of these products can be broken down by sunlight, so finding an agent designed for use in the yard is necessary.

It is always important to follow all the precautions on the spray's label to avoid toxicity to you and your pet and to avoid run-off into lakes and streams. Concentrate your efforts in areas where your pet spends most of his time, remembering the types of environments the flea prefers.

In the home, a similar plan should also be used. Vacuuming the house and disposing of the bag outdoors is an important first step.

Wash the pet's bedding in hot water. Again, when treating the home, use a product that kills both adults and immature fleas and blocks the ongoing life cycle. By blocking the continuation of the life cycle, treatment of the home can be performed less frequently. Concentrate your treatments in the areas your pet is found most often, but do treat the entire house, including closets, attics, basements, porches, and crawl spaces. Make sure a spray is used under furniture, including after the use of foggers.

If foggers are used, one is needed for every room including hallways, as the fog will not go around corners. Bearing in mind the short life cycle under ideal conditions, the treatments need to be spaced two weeks apart at first in heavy infestations.

Should your cat display signs of infectious disease, it is essential to thoroughly wash all bedding (including your own) to avoid transmitting the disease to other members of the family.

Maintenance treatments can occur months apart with the proper product. Again, follow all safety precautions on the labels of all materials used and protect all pets from exposure, including fish tanks and bird cages.

Products for use with your pet have made the most significant recent advances. Shampoos can be used weekly, but some products can be drying, and most have a very short duration of effectiveness. Dips may last longer but cannot be used as often due to potential toxicity. Powders and spot-on products are available also. There are numerous sprays and foams on the market, most of which kill adult fleas and vary in the duration of action on the pet.

The length of time these products work can vary depending on the formulation of the product, environmental conditions, and degree of flea infestation. Flea collars exist in a wide range of types with a large variation in reported effectiveness. Shampoos and sprays can be effective and useful first steps in addressing a flea problem. Some of the newer products state that they are effective in damaging the flea eggs before and after falling off of the pet's body. This would be helpful in breaking the continuing cycle. One product in the form of a monthly pill or liquid affects the development of the flea by entering the egg while it is in the female flea and essentially preventing the development of new fleas.

The newest "on-pet" products are designed to last several weeks and come as a spray or liquid that is placed on the pet's neck or back and spread over the body. These products are designed to kill the adults before they bite, preventing the production of eggs as well as the reaction to the flea bite. The duration and effectiveness of these materials may be affected by frequency of bathing and by the condition of the skin.

Repellents in the form of different fragrances are thought to be useful in preventing the feeding by the flea, and subsequent egg production. Numerous products on the market have success rates that vary by individual and have not been extensively researched through scientific study. The product to use on your pet depends on individual environments, types of pets in the household, and your ability to perform the necessary tasks. Cats are particularly sensitive to many drugs and sprays.

It is important to consult with your veterinarian concerning flea control. Read product labels carefully, and make sure you use products that are specifically approved for use with cats. Some products are safe and can be used with both dogs and cats. Potential reintroduction of fleas into a treated area may also affect product use. In addition to reintroduction of fleas, another common reason for breakdowns in flea control may be due to the persistence of the most resistant stage, which is the adult inside the cocoon.

TICKS

Ticks are another type of insect that may feed on the blood of your pet. They can be a source of infection by certain parasites, viruses, fungi, bacteria, and other pathogenic organisms that may cause diseases. There are four stages of the life cycle of the most common classification of ticks: In addition to the egg and the adult, there is a larval stage and a nymph stage, both of which must feed completely before detaching from the pet and molting to the next stage. The adult may increase its weight one hundred times while feeding and can produce thousands of eggs after detachment.

There is a risk of life-threatening anemia with massive tick infestation. The greatest risk of infection from the diseases that may be carried by ticks occurs when the tick is infected at the youngest possible stage, such as the egg or larval stage. The disease is passed to subsequent stages, all of which feed on the host, increasing the chance of transmitting the disease to your pet.

The saliva from ticks, in addition to the unusual possibility of causing a severe whole body disease, can affect the body's immune system at that site, allowing infection to occur. The bite itself is painless, allowing the tick to stay attached, undetected by its host. This time frame allows for feeding as well as the transmission of any disease the tick is carrying. In some instances, the bite site can become irritated by the local infection or a reaction to the mouth parts of the tick, causing the pet to scratch repeatedly in the area.

Ticks are attracted by motion, heat, carbon dioxide,

This cat suffers from ear mites, which had a secondary effect of causing milliary dermatitis on other parts of the body.

and changes in light. They do not jump or fly and rely on direct contact to get onto the pet. Therefore avoidance is the best method of preventing tick problems. Should a tick attach to your pet's skin, prompt removal is required. This may be done with fine-pointed tweezers or any number of tick removal devices that get as close as possible to the skin surface and gently pull the tick free.

The types of ticks with strong mouth parts may take a tiny piece of the animal's skin when removed, and ones with fragile mouth parts may leave fragments of these parts behind. Both situations may cause localized irritation. The area should be cleaned with soap and water to prevent infection. The person removing the tick should wear gloves and avoid contact with the insect. Petroleum jelly, matches, and other such home remedies are not effective and may make the situation worse.

Ticks may be killed by any number of the flea products discussed previously, and the label on each will reveal its effectiveness. Environmental control may be achieved on a limited basis through sprays. Elimination of other hosts such as deer and rodents has not been successful in controlling ticks. As was discussed under the topic of flea control, cats are particularly sensitive to many drugs and sprays.

Consultation with your veterinarian concerning tick control measures and reading product labels carefully are absolute necessities. It is important to use only products that are specifically approved for use with cats, although some products can be safely used on both cats and dogs.

INTERNAL PARASITES

Internal parasites do not normally cause problems in the skin. If they do, it is usually by affecting the

overall health of the body. They may make a pet more susceptible to skin infections or may affect the normal healthy biology of the skin. In some cases, these internal parasites may find their way to the skin and cause sores, rashes, or itching.

If a patient has intestinal parasites in addition to skin problems, various test results may be affected. Both for general health purposes and to obtain a clearer picture of what is causing a skin problem, it is often advisable to test for and treat these internal parasites if present.

Until recently, heartworm-associated disease was not thought to be a significant problem in cats. New information suggests that it may be more common than previously thought. A link between skin disease and feline heartworm has not yet been established.

MITES AND MANGE

Most mites are so small

Your veterinarian will keep close tabs on your cat's health, and strive to keep your pet in optimal health.

that their presence can be confirmed only through the use of a microscope. The most common mites seen in cats include ear mites (*Otodectes cynotis*), feline scabies (*Notoedres cati*), and in some parts of the world, "walking dandruff" (*Cheyletiella* mites) and fur mites (*lynxacarus radovskyi*). *Demodex* mites are increasingly recognized in association with skin disease.

Ear mites is perhaps the most commonly diagnosed mite. The use of the term is somewhat confusing because the mites may also be found on other parts of the body as well as in the ear canal. Ear problems may also be caused by other relatively common diseases. Allergies to airborne allergens or food may also result in similar symptoms.

Typical symptoms of an ear mite infestation include the accumulation of dark brown to black material that resembles coffee grounds. Itching is often overwhelming, especially about the face. Intense facial itching is also commonly seen with food allergy. With both diseases, other parts of the body, such as the neck and rump, may also be affected with itching and/or miliary dermatitis.

Itching and irritation may be due to the mites themselves or because of the cat's allergic response to the mites and their droppings. Some of the most itchy cats may actually have a relatively low number of mites but can be very allergic to the few mites that are present. The mites are highly contagious and can affect cats as well as dogs. Some cats can be carriers of the mite, yet show virtually no symptoms of infestation.

However, in most cases, the diagnosis is relatively easy to confirm by examining the debris from the ear or skin under a microscope. Occasionally it is difficult to find the mites, and the diagnosis is made by monitoring response to therapy. All animals in the household or those who regularly come in contact with the affected patient should also be examined and treated for ear mites.

Treatment involves cleaning out the ears and then applying products that will kill the ear mites. Therapy that is directed only at the ear may result in an incomplete cure. Initial improvement may be noted, but mites from other parts of the body may reinfest the ear. The result is an initial improvement, followed by a relapse, especially after treatment is discontinued. It is advisable to use a flea powder or spray (which is labeled safe for cats) on the entire body. The egg of the mite is rather resistant to virtually all forms of treatment.

The mites are so geared up for reproduction that they begin breeding within minutes of hatching from their eggs. In order to prevent these newly hatched mites from continuing to produce more mites, treatment should be continued for 28 days. "Pulse therapy," consisting of ten days of treatment, followed by ten days without treatment and then ten more days of treatment, is also an option. The use of ivermectin has revolutionized the treatment of ear mites. It has been used successfully both by topical administration directly to the ears and by injection. The injectable route is associated with a faster cure and fewer relapses. It is often many veterinary dermatologists' first choice in treating this disease because of its efficacy, ease of administration (especially when multiple animals are affected) and the extremely low incidence of side effects. However, this drug has not been approved by the FDA for use in cats even though it has rarely been associated with

The demodex mite can be passed from the queen to her kittens.

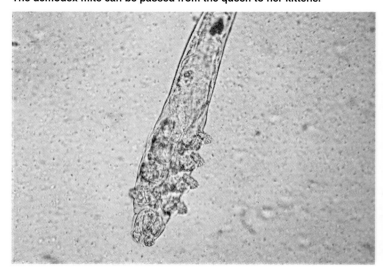

life-threatening reactions.

In summary, virtually all cats with ear problems should be tested for ear mites. If mites are not found, it may be prudent to appropriately treat for mites to make sure that they are not present in very small numbers. Other cats and dogs in the household may also require treatment. If the ear problems persist, other diseases such as allergies, immune-mediated diseases, and viral diseases such as FeLV and FIV should be considered.

Cheyletiella mites are a relatively common mite, especially in some climates where flea products are not routinely used on a regular basis. They may affect the entire body but seem to prefer the region along the back from the neck to the rump. This may be similar to the symptoms of other diseases. In many cases, the itching is a predominant symptom, but in some cases it is absent.

Like ear mites, the mites themselves can cause itching, but many animals actually develop an allergy to the mites and their droppings. In these animals, a small number of mites can cause severe symptoms. *Cheyletiella* mites are very contagious and may live in the environment for many days without the presence of a pet. Some cats and dogs may harbor these mites without showing any significant symptoms. Humans may also be transiently affected, which may cause red bumps and spots on the skin. These mites are not able to perpetuate their life cycle and species while on a human, but they can cause discomfort. If you

Should your cat exhibit excessive scratching and licking, it is often indicative of an allergy or the presence of an irritation or skin infection.

A diet that includes pure protein sources and other wholesome ingredients can give your cat the nutrients he needs for overall good health—a condition that's reflected in supple skin and a lustrous, full coat. Photo courtesy of Nature's Recipe Pet Foods.

suspect that these mites may be causing a problem on yourself or other human members of the household, consult a dermatologist. In general, specific species of mites prefer to live on specific species of animal. However, the mite that affects dogs may also affect cats and vice-versa. The rabbit mite may also affect multiple species of animals.

In some cases, with the use of a magnifying glass, the mite can actually be seen on the pet, moving among the dandruff and flakes. This is likely where the term "walking dandruff" originated. Often it is necessary for a veterinarian to examine the flakes and scales to observe the mites. Actual mite numbers may be so small that their presence cannot be confirmed, especially in a cat who had developed an allergy to the mites. This can make it even more difficult to differentiate this relatively easily treated disease from other more complex diseases.

"Empirical treatment" or appropriately treating and monitoring for a response to therapy may be necessary in some cases. This method is the least desirable method of confirming the disease because other diseases with similar symptoms may wax and wane, and thus falsely give the impression of improvement due to therapy for mites.

Therapy may consist of "dips," which are sponged-on applications of diluted antiparasitic medications that are not rinsed off after use. Dips are effective in many cases, but may be unpleasant and tedious to apply, and

require repeated applications on a weekly basis.

A commonly recommended therapy for *Cheyletiella* infestation is lime sulfur dips. However, this product has a strong odor and is tedious to appropriately apply, especially in multi-cat households. Ivermectin is fast becoming the treatment of choice, but it is not approved by the FDA for use in this manner. The pet's environment should also be treated because of this mite's ability to live off animals for several days. Most environmental flea products are effective.

In summary, in certain geographic regions, it is important to make sure that a cat's skin disease is not caused by these mites. Like ear mites, if the mites are not found, it may be prudent to appropriately treat for the mites to make sure that they are not present in very small numbers. Other cats and dogs in the household may also require treatment in addition to environmental treatment. If the problem persists in spite of therapy, diseases such as allergies, ringworm, and other possibilities such as FeLV and FIV should be considered.

Scabies mites (*Notoedres cati*) are similar to the scabies mite that affects dogs. They are very contagious. Intense itching and self-trauma are the primary symptoms. The face, margins of the ears, elbows, and stomach region are the most commonly affected areas. In advanced cases, thick crust can accumulate. Although it is likely that an allergic response to the mite will occur, these mites are typically more easily found

than with some other mite infestations. Scabies infestation is potentially highly contagious, but not all animals that are exposed to the affected pet will become affected themselves. Some may actually harbor the mites on their bodies, but not show any symptoms.

Typical clinical signs include extreme itching and crusts on the margins of the ear. However, some animals will be affected in different areas or may only show signs of itching without any crusts, redness, or hair loss. The human scabies mite is different than the cat scabies mite and is generally believed not to be transmissible from humans to cats or to dogs. Treatment may consist of various topical dips to the "extra-lable use" of ivermectin. Although the potential side effects of ivermectin can be life threatening, it is often the therapy of choice in treating an infestation of *Notoedres* mites.

With either therapy, all cats that have contact with the infested cat should be treated. When compared with dogs, the use of ivermectin in cats appears to be associated with a much lower chance of side effects. However, it should not be used indiscriminately. Environmental treatment is usually not necessary because the parasite cannot live off animals for very long.

Demodex mites come in two different varieties for cats. *Demodex cati* is similar to the dog *Demodex* mite but is more slender. This mite lives in the hair follicles and low numbers of them is considered "normal." This number is so low that routine skin scrapes on a pet that does not show any symptoms will almost always be negative or perhaps yield only one mite. (Skin scrapes involve scraping the skin and removing a small amount of debris for examination under the microscope.)

Demodex cati is not considered to be contagious. The second type of Demodex mite that affects cats is shorter and more stubby in appearance. It has not yet been given a name. We know less about this mite and its behavior. In general, it appears more likely to cause itching than does Demodex cati, and some veterinary dermatologists suspect that there is a chance that it is potentially contagious.

Cats may show clinical signs associated with the presence of these mites, such as patchy hair loss on the face, neck, and legs, with or without itching. Sometimes, other areas of the body are affected. Redness and small scabs or crust may be present. Occasionally, the mites may only be associated with the ear canal and ear problems. Mild cases affecting a single or limited areas of skin are referred to as having localized demodicosis. More severe cases that affect several areas or even the whole body are referred to as having generalized demodicosis. Siamese and Burmese cats may be more predisposed than other breeds toward the development of the generalized form. Genetic predisposition, general ill health, and the use of drugs that suppress the immune system, such as steroids, can contribute to

generalized demodicosis.

Localized demodicosis is self-limiting and will often go away on its own or with a relatively mild treatment. Generalized demodicosis caused by Demodex cati is treated differently than the localized disease caused by this mite. An underlying

disease may have compromised a cat's immune system. Blood work, including a CBC/Chemistry and feline leukemia virus and feline immunodeficiency virus testing, is advisable. Treatment recommendations for this disease are still evolving.

Today's veterinarian and dermatology specialist have an entire arsenal of defense in combating skin disease and allergies. Diagnostic testing offers a window of opportunity in terms of isolating the source of the illness.

It's fine for these two playful cats to scratch their post, but the pet owner should take immediate action if they begin to scratch their skin.

LICE

The diagnosis of lice in small animals is becoming increasingly rare. This is due in part to the use of flea control products that are usually very effective in eliminating lice. These parasites, unlike mites, are usually large enough so that they or their eggs are visible to the naked eye. The type of louse that affects humans is different from the type that affects dogs; the louse that affects cats is yet another type. In other words, these different types of lice affect only a specific type of animal. Lice can cause inflammation of the skin and profound itching but are usually easily treated with one of many products designed to kill fleas.

CHIGGERS AND MOSQUITOES

A variety of other parasites ranging from chiggers to mosquitoes can cause skin problems in animals. Chiggers affect animals and people for only a short period of time and may appear as very small bright orange dots that are best noticed with a magnifying glass. Fortunately, they respond to many forms of flea control as well as to "giving them time to go away on their own." Mosquitoes have been associated with an unusual syndrome in response to their bites. Sores and bumps may be seen primarily on the animal's head in less-haired regions.

In summary, most common parasitic problems are relatively easily diagnosed and treated. In many cases, they can complicate the diagnosis and treatment of other skin problems.

Above: These two cats from the same household have contracted chiggers. *Below:* Chiggers is a condition that can cause intense itching and skin discomfort, as indicated by this close-up photo.

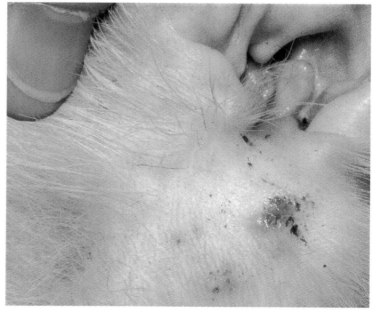

To keep your cat looking fit and healthy, be sure to contact your veterinarian at the first sign of illness.

ALLERGIES AND ITCHING

Allergies are often a chronic, incurable, but controllable disease. Most cats with allergies exhibit problems in the skin, but allergies may sometimes cause ear problems or be associated with breathing problems. This is a frustrating group of diseases that requires dedication and commitment on the part of the human members of the household.

Itching and scratching at night may prevent a good night's rest for people and pets in the house. Respiratory problems can be life-threatening and warrant emergency treatment. The

Although chronic in nature, allergies can oftentimes be controlled, allowing your cat to lead a happy and comfortable life.

poor quality of life for a severely allergic pet, or the side effects and cost of treatment may lead some pet owners to become distraught and angry. This anger may be directed towards the breeder, other human members of the household, the health care provider, or the patient. Understanding the complex, chronic, incurable, yet often controllable nature of allergies should help you deal with these frustrations and enable you to improve the quality of your pet's life.

Allergies and itching often go hand in hand. Itching has been defined as a sensation that provokes the desire to scratch. An itchy animal may also lick, chew, or groom itself excessively. Some pets may demonstrate these signs only when they are alone. A pet that is uncomfortable may also exhibit behavioral changes. Psychological factors can contribute to the nature and extent of the symptoms. The degree of itching can be so severe that the skin may become irritated, sore, and infected. In addition to allergies (flea, inhalant, food, and contact), other potential causes of itching include parasites (fleas, mites, and lice), infections (bacterial and fungal), and other less common, but potentially life-threatening diseases.

The single most important aspect in controlling the

Allergies and itching often occur simultaneously.

itching sensation is to identify and treat the underlying problem. This is especially true in severe or chronic cases. Evaluation by a veterinarian or a veterinary dermatologist is an important step to take to identify contributing factors and begin treatment.

Some causes of itching respond quickly to therapy, while others do not. Often, several contributing factors may be present in a single pet. This is important to understand because of the concept of "summation of effect" and the "threshold concept of itching." This means that a single factor alone may not necessarily cause itching, but when two factors are present at the same time, the sum of them reaches the threshold, and an itch will become noticeable. For instance, a pet may be able to tolerate a small number of fleas without a problem, but during a particular time of year when certain pollen allergies are present, itching may be a problem. Or if fleas were not present, itching may not be a problem during that time of the year.

Another common scenario is the allergic patient whose itching is well controlled with immunotherapy injections but whose itching flares up tremendously when specific additional pollens are present. In other words, the immunotherapy injections have helped bring the level of itch-producing factors below the itch threshold, but during a particular time of year when a certain pollen count is high, the level of itch-producing factors rises above the threshold and the symptoms reappear. Some patients may even be able to tolerate two or three different factors adequately without itching,

only to flare-up when an additional factor is present.

Another example is noted when an allergic animal may be well-controlled with immunotherapy injections until a psychologically stressful situation causes an increase in licking, which then promotes a self-perpetuating cycle. The associated stress factors add to the other factors contributing to the itch resulting a "summation of effect," which exceeds the pet's "itch threshold" and itching results.

Another possibility is that stress may lower the threshold for itching. Prior to this, the summation of the itch-causing factors may not have been great enough to

reach the threshold and result in clinical signs. However, when the threshold is lowered, the same factors that did not previously cause problems could then result in a disorder.

The treatment of allergies is often a lifetime commitment, and it is advisable to evaluate the possibility of additional, or coexisting, diseases. Occasionally, it may be necessary to repeatedly test for the presence of these other diseases because some diseases may occur spontaneously, and some treatments may predispose a patient to certain diseases.

Depending on the history of your pet's illness, it may be advisable to rule out some or all of these other causes of

This cat's lip has become enlarged, a condition often associated with allergic conditions.

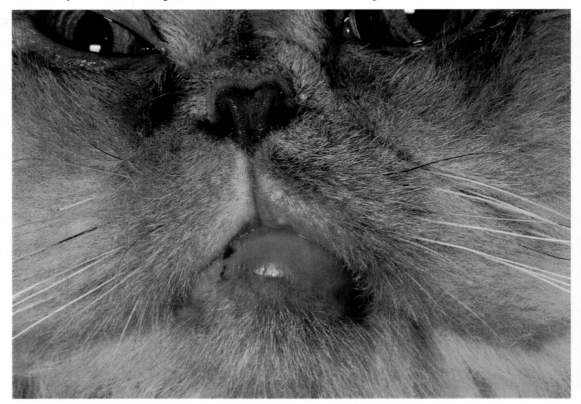

There is cause for concern if you notice that your cat's habitual licking occurs beyond his normal grooming behavior.

itching. Many of these other causes, as well as potentially coexisting disease may complicate the diagnosis and therapy. Many types of skin disease look very much alike, having only subtle differences in appearance and historical background. This chapter will present an in-depth discussion of allergies and briefly touch on other factors that can cause itching. Many of these other factors are discussed in more detail elsewhere in this book.

COMPLICATING FACTORS

Fleas

The most common parasite to cause itching is the flea. Although some animals may harbor large numbers of fleas without any apparent discomfort, the presence of fleas and their associated flea bites alone will cause most pets to exhibit some degree of itching. In these cases, they may lick, chew, or rub their tail, back, rump, thighs, or neck area.

Other diseases can have similar symptoms. Many cats may also be allergic to the flea saliva. In this case, a single flea and its associated flea bites can make them miserable. Flea allergy dermatitis is one of the most itchy dermatological diseases affecting cats. It can be difficult to determine how much of a pet's skin problem is due to fleas and how much is due to another disease until the flea situation is controlled.

Human members of the household may think that a few fleas are not a problem, but a pet may have a problem with the few numbers of fleas that are present. Sometimes, small numbers of fleas may be a problem—without human detection. This is especially true in cats who groom themselves so well that they may remove the fleas from their body very quickly.

Mites and Lice

Most mites are so small that their presence can only be confirmed through the use of a microscope. Most of these infestations can be relatively easily diagnosed and treated. A pet's history, response to past treatment, physical examination results and microscopic evaluation should all be considered before pursuing a complete allergy workup. Some cats may have had allergies that had previously been well-controlled for years through the use of steroids. However, the steroids may seem to have lost their effectiveness. This is sometimes the a result of side effects associated with excessive steroid use.

Infections (Ringworm and Bacteria)

Various infections can also cause skin problems. As was previously discussed, such medications as steroids can predispose a pet to skin infections, either as a result of the steroids themselves or by excessive steroid use, as is the case with diabetes.

MANIFESTATIONS OF ALLERGY IN THE CAT

The clinical signs associated with allergies in cats are varied. They may range from a severe to a moderate itch or the appearance of excessive grooming. A crusty dermatitis and/or hairless area may also be present. The term "miliary dermatitis" is often used to describe this symptom. The gritty texture of debris on the surface of the skin is usually

Many skin problems are the result of food allergies, which can be minimized by careful analysis of and attention to the ingredients in your cat's diet. High-quality ingredients typically result in fewer problems. Photo courtesy of Nature's Recipe Pet Foods.

easier to feel than see. It is important to note that miliary dermatitis is actually a symptom and not a disease. Many different skin diseases can cause the symptoms of miliary dermatitis. In some cats, sores, ulcers, or scabs may develop on the lip, back of the legs, or skin of the stomach, which may or may not itch. The terms eosinophilic granuloma, eosinophilic ulcer (rodent ulcer), and eosinophilic plaque are often used to describe these symptoms.

As with miliary dermatitis, these terms should be considered as symptoms of a disease and an underlying cause should be determined. Diseases other than allergies may also be present. In addition to dermatological symptoms, behavioral changes including irritability, aggressiveness, nervousness, and other symptoms may be seen with allergies.

The most common types of allergies found in cats include flea allergy, inhalant allergy (similar to hay fever in humans), and food allergy. Contact allergy is quite rare. The hallmark clinical signs of allergies are itching, licking, or excessive grooming. Often these different types of allergies may have symptoms that look alike with only subtle differences in history, distribution of clinical signs, or response to therapy.

Fungal (ringworm) infections and mite or flea infestations may also mimic the clinical signs of allergies. The basic physiological aspect of different types of allergies is similar: The allergy-causing substance gains entrance into the body either through the skin, lungs, or digestive tract. In normal animals, these substances (called allergens) do not cause the individual any problems. In affected animals, the allergens cause an abnormal immune response, resulting in various clinical signs.

In many cases, fleas complicate the task of identifying other causes of itching, such as allergies. Often, a pet's itching may be due to a combination of fleas and other factors. The clinical signs of allergic inhalant dermatitis and food allergy can be very similar to symptoms linked to flea-associated dermatitis. Many people are under the false impression that if fleas or flea bites do not affect humans, fleas are not a problem for their pet. Most fleas prefer dogs and cats to humans.

Mild to moderate flea infestations may not actually result in a problem for humans in the house, but a relatively few number of fleas can cause a significant problem for the animals in the house. If adequate flea control is not effective in controlling itching, other possible causes should be considered.

Flea Allergy

In contrast to the non-flea-allergic cat that itches only when exposed to several fleas, a flea-allergic cat can suffer from extreme discomfort associated with a single flea. The flea allergy reaction occurs when a flea bites a flea-allergic cat and exposes the cat's immune system to flea saliva. The ensuing allergic reaction can occur very quickly and may also last for many days. Clinical signs are often more severe near the area of the flea bite but can also occur in distant

This photo demonstrates how skin testing can determine the source of your cat's allergies.

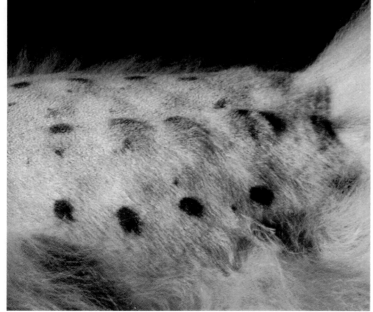

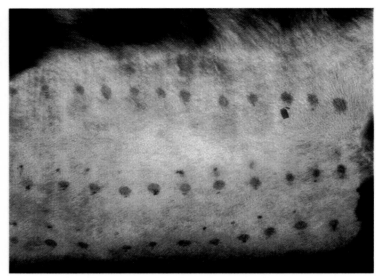

The red and swollen areas in this photo denote reactions to allergy agents.

locations (such as the neck and head). Itching, redness, miliary dermatitis, symptoms of eosinophilic granuloma complex, and self-induced trauma may manifest themselves. As with flea infestation, the most severely affected area is often on or near the rump and neck region. Excessive licking or chewing of other parts of the body can be seen with flea allergy as well as other allergies.

Eradication of fleas is the most important aspect of controlling a flea-allergic cat. Cats are more sensitive than dogs to certain flea products that are applied directly on them. It is important to use only products that specifically state that they are safe for use on cats when implementing a flea control program. Consultation with a veterinarian concerning potential toxicities and effectiveness is strongly recommended when implementing any flea control program.

Allergic Inhalant Dermatitis

Allergic inhalant dermatitis is also called atopy. This disease involves allergic reactions to various pollens (grasses, trees, molds, and weeds) as well as other substances with microscopic allergens that can be inhaled, such as dust and dust mites. These substances interact with the cat's immune system primarily through the lungs.

Humans with inhalant allergies primarily suffer from symptoms such as runny noses, irritated eyes, and sneezing. Cats usually manifest this type of allergy by scratching, rubbing, licking, biting, or excessively grooming themselves. The rump, neck, and skin of the abdominal region are commonly affected. Some cats develop a crusty dermatitis or miliary dermatitis, which may or may not itch. Red sores that weep or ooze (associated with eosinophilic granuloma complex affecting the lips and other parts of the body), may be seen with inhalant

allergies. The symptoms may start after the age of adolescence and initially cause problems during a particular season. With time, the clinical signs become more severe and may last all year long.

It is possible to control exposure to the allergens that cause flea, food, and contact allergy, but it is difficult to control exposure to substances in the air. If the clinical signs cause the pet to be uncomfortable, medical therapy may be necessary. If the symptoms do not adequately respond to medical therapy or side effects of the drugs occur, allergy testing should be considered.

Currently, two different methods for allergy testing exist. Skin testing for allergies involves the intradermal injection of small amounts of various types of diluted purified allergen extracts and monitoring for a wheal (a localized reaction that looks like a welt). Skin testing, or intradermal skin testing as it is also known, is similar to the allergy test that most people are familiar with. Blood testing is a relatively new type of test that involves obtaining a sample of blood and submitting it to a specialized testing laboratory.

After the positive reactions identified with the allergy test are correlated with the history, the immunotherapy solution (allergy extract) can be formulated. This solution contains a mixture of specific allergens. The exact mix of allergens is different for each patient, and is based upon the pet's history, positive allergy test results, the

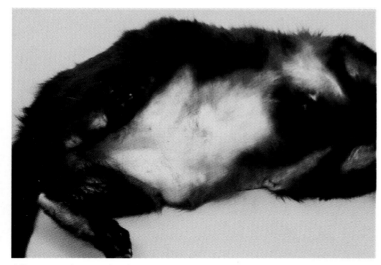

Allergy testing, and subsequent treatment, can help contain the level of discomfort experienced by your cat, and vastly improve your cat's quality of life.

The less accurate nature of using groups or mixes for allergy testing complicates the formulation of the immunotherapy solution and may inadvertently lead to omission of an important allergen in the allergy extract. Additionally, the practice of using groups or mixes could lead to the inclusion of allergens that are not relevant, thereby diluting the concentration of the important allergens. Both situations are likely to reduce the efficacy of the treatment.

Studies with dogs indicate that the highest success rate with immunotherapy is achieved through the use of the most precise testing and the highest concentration of immunotherapy solution. Grouping of allergens should be avoided in either type of allergy test, and the highest concentration of immunotherapy solution that can safely be used should be administered as an allergy shot.

Skin testing allows for

veterinarian's (and/or the laboratory's) clinical experience in treating allergies, and other considerations. Injections of immunotherapy solution of allergy extract are also referred to as allergy shots. This type of allergy shot should not be confused with steroid or cortisone injections, which are quite different.

The treatment of allergies is complicated, and the likelihood of success with immunotherapy (or allergy shots) can be affected by a number of factors. The most precise results are obtained with the use of individual allergens rather than groups of allergens. The disadvantage in using groups of mixed allergens becomes apparent when considering the results of the test. When a group of mixed allergens has a negative test, all allergens in the group or mix are considered to be negative. This is unfortunate because if

the allergens were tested individually, one of the allergens could actually show a true positive test result. Conversely, a group of mixed allergens that test positive may actually contain an individual allergen that would truly test negative if individual testing were performed.

Allergy shots, while not a cure-all, are recommended in certain circumstances, as a treatment for specific allergies.

relatively inexpensive identification of individual allergens. It also involves testing the organ of the body (the skin) that is showing symptoms of the disease. Many blood tests are also at a disadvantage because they test for groups or mixes of allergens. Although it is possible to utilize groups or mixes of allergens with skin testing, most allergens are tested individually. The concentration of the immunotherapy (allergy extract) solution can also vary with the type of test performed and, as previously discussed, can affect the success rate.

Skin testing has numerous advantages over blood testing but is complicated to perform and interpret. Both types of test are best performed under the guidance of a veterinarian with specialized training in the treatment of allergic skin diseases. In summary,

intradermal skin testing is the historical standard and the preferred method for allergy testing. Some veterinary dermatologists find the combined use of both tests to be useful.

If a pet is diagnosed as having allergic inhalant dermatitis, there are several different methods of therapy. The first is to remove the offending allergen from the animal's environment. Unfortunately, this is not possible in most instances. The second method involves the use of drugs or medications. In general, an adequate response to medical therapy, not including steroids, is noted in approximately 20-30 percent of patients with allergic inhalant dermatitis. Each pet is different, and different regions of the country and the world will likely exhibit different response rates. Various types and

combinations of medications may be tried until the best one is determined. Medications usually result in relatively quick improvement, while immunotherapy injections may take 3-12 months or more until improvement is noted. Many pet owners find administering the immunotherapy injections every two-four weeks to be far more convenient than daily or twice daily administration of pills or liquid.

Immunotherapy injections, or allergy shots, consist of a series of diluted allergens that are given to change a pet's immune system and render it less sensitive to allergies. They are helpful in approximately 75 percent of the patients seen by a board-certified veterinary dermatologist and allergy tested using an intradermal skin test. Most pet owners are able to learn how to give these injections.

Adhering to strict dietary guidelines plays a vital role in the management of food sensitivities.

Food Allergy

Food allergy is a relatively rare disease and is generally overemphasized by many pet food companies as a cause of itching. Intense itching of the face and head is a common symptom, but the clinical signs can be virtually indistinguishable from those seen in allergic inhalant dermatitis. Itchy cats should be evaluated for mites because mite infestation may mimic food allergy. The symptoms are *not* usually associated with a change in diet, may start at any age, and do not vary with the time of year or season.

Various tests may become available for assistance in diagnosing food allergy in cats. However, neither blood tests nor skin tests are very helpful in confirming the diagnosis in dogs. While positive reactions are seen often, they are usually not clinically important. False positive reactions may lead to the incorrect assumption that a pet is very food allergic. Negative reactions offer slightly more useful information and indicate that a pet can likely tolerate a specific food substance.

Most veterinary dermatologists do not recommend blood tests or skin tests for the diagnosis of food allergy in dogs and cats. The best way to diagnose a food allergy is with the proper use of a hypoallergenic diet. This diet should be based on a pet's previous dietary history so that the meat and grains that have been previously eaten regularly may be avoided. Manufacturer claims that a diet contains certain

An allergic cat often feels "itchy" from head to toe.

substances does not indicate that the diet is truly hypoallergenic.

In order for an animal to be allergic to a food substance, the animal must have been exposed to the substance before. Lamb is a good example. There is absolutely nothing magical about lamb and food allergy. Simply, most pets have not eaten lamb before and therefore cannot be allergic to it. A cat that has eaten lamb as part of its normal diet may actually be allergic to lamb. For years, lamb has been recommended by veterinarians as an alternative protein source for beef or chicken in the diet of pets suspected of having food allergy. Unfortunately, the indiscriminate use of lamb in many cat foods has further complicated the necessary steps required to diagnose food allergy.

Some foods advertised as

"lamb and rice" also contain corn and poultry by-products as well as other potential allergens commonly found in more "routine" types of diets. A well-meaning pet owner may try to perform a hypoallergenic dietary trial by changing from a "routine" diet to one of the "lamb and rice" diets, which also contain food substances to which the pet may actually be allergic. Careful reading of ingredient lists and a consultation with a veterinarian or veterinary dermatologist is often helpful in avoiding this mistake.

Before initiating a hypoallergenic diet, a pet owner must understand that it is a true diagnostic test and should not be undertaken without conviction. Many times a hypoallergenic dietary trial is not strictly followed, and the pet is allowed continued exposure to table scraps or beef-flavored treats

If you own an allergy-prone cat, choose a cat food that is formulated with alternative food sources.

diagnosing food allergy. An improperly managed hypoallergenic dietary trial may actually do more harm than good because it may complicate future attempts to diagnose food allergy. Diets containing certain substances such as lamb are not necessarily hypoallergenic. The hypoallergenic diet should be continued until the cat improves or for a duration of 8 to 10 weeks. If a pet improves while on a hypoallergenic diet, the original diet should be reintroduced and the pet monitored for the return of symptoms within 7 to 14 days. Sometimes symptoms may return within a matter of hours. This reintroduction of the original diet is a critical part of the test and helps prove that the improvement was due to the food and not coincidence.

Once a food allergy is confirmed in this manner, the patient should be put back on the successful hypoallergenic diet until the itching is no longer present. The cat can be maintained on this diet (provided it is well balanced and complete) or placed on

and toys. Vitamin supplements that contain meat flavorings should be substituted with a comparable product that does not contain these potential allergens.

Failure to observe these requirements invalidates the test and results in unnecessarily exposing the pet to another potentially allergenic substance, such as lamb. This unnecessary exposure may preclude the use of such substances from being utilized in the future, when a stricter hypoallergenic diet is considered.

In summary, a properly

managed hypoallergenic dietary trial is the most appropriate test for

To keep your cat looking his best, you need to feed him a food that is high in digestibility, one that contains the highest quality ingredients—and one your cat will enjoy! Your cat's good health will show from the inside out. Photo courtesy of Nature's Recipe Pet Foods.

another diet and monitored for recurrence of itching. The introduction of potential allergenic substances may also be added individually to the proven hypoallergenic diet. This protocol allows for more precise identification of the offending food substance.

In some animals with both inhalant allergies and food allergies, it may be necessary to institute the hypoallergenic diet during the winter months, when fewer inhalant allergens are present.

TREATMENT FOR THE ALLERGIC CAT

The identification and treatment of allergies in cats can be both frustrating and challenging. It is important to ensure that other diseases that mimic allergies are not present. Non-specific medical control of allergies can be helpful while investigating what type of allergy is present. Cats tend to tolerate steroids better than dogs, but side effects can occur. Hormonal drugs such as Ovoban should be avoided because of their potential to cause diabetes and mammary tumors. The use of medications (antihistamines and fatty acids) should be considered and discussed with a veterinarian or veterinary dermatologist.

It is important to remember that more than one disease may be contributing to itching. If identification and treatment for one of the causes does not result in adequate improvement, other causes should also be considered. Sometimes, the treatment of a specific disease may require some time to become effective. In these situations, or in cases involving an unidentified cause, nonspecific treatment for itching should be considered. Both topical therapy (shampoos, sprays, lotions, and creams) and systemic therapy (medications given by mouth) can be useful.

The use of drugs other than steroids to control itching is less convenient but reduces the potential for serious side effects, especially when long-term therapy is needed. If these other drugs are not totally effective in controlling clinical signs, they often reduce the amount of steroids that are necessary to decrease itching. Some patients require a combination of immunotherapy injections, antihistamines, fatty acids, and even intermittent steroids in order to maintain an adequate comfort level without incurring side effects due to overuse of one drug.

The cost of antihistamines and fatty acids is usually greater than the cost of steroids. However, the cost of side effects and diseases associated with excessive steroid use can be substantial in terms of money and health.

Your cat is not the only one who will require treatment should a flea infestation arise. Every square inch of his environment, including his bed, your house and yard must be treated as well.

OTHER COMMON PROBLEMS

Many different types of diseases can affect the skin—directly and indirectly. There are various ways to classify skin problems or symptoms. Classically, diseases are grouped by their cause. However, it may be equally important to consider other factors.

For the patient's and pet owner's sake, it is often appropriate to group diseases based on the likelihood the presence of a particular disease. Additionally, the cost and invasiveness of the tests that may be necessary to confirm a diagnosis are often a consideration. The length of time that may be required to confirm the diagnosis and/or achieve a cure is also a factor.

The presence of a concurrent disease or complicating factors may affect the recommended treatments and the order in which diagnostic tests are performed. Some symptoms may be the result of a disease that causes skin problems as well as problems in other parts of the body (such as internal organs). It may be helpful to group diseases according to their history and to which symptoms occurred first (itching, a rash, or hair loss). Often, the symptoms have been present for so long or are so varied that it may be difficult to remember the progression of the disease.

Various skin problems look very much alike. Fortunately,

the more common ones, such as most infections or mite infestations, either respond relatively quickly to treatment or do not require particularly invasive or expensive tests to confirm the diagnosis. These diseases may be present by themselves or in association with other more complex and difficult-to-treat (and diagnose) diseases. It may be necessary to treat the more common and straightforward disease before pursuing further diagnostic tests or treatments. In some situations, it is necessary to treat for several suspected and confirmed diseases at the same time in a single patient. The possibility that the overall general health of the body

An entire veterinary specialty is devoted exclusively to pet's skin care.

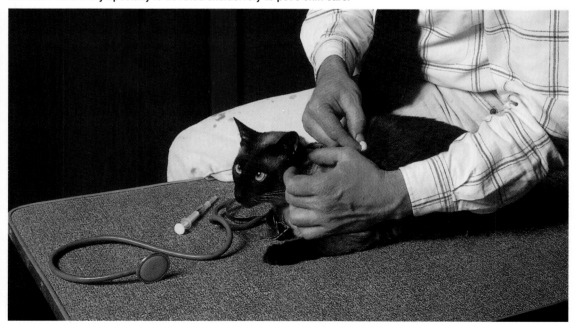

may be compromised suggests that tests be performed to rule out such diseases as diabetes, liver or kidney abnormalities, or problems with red or white blood cells.

INFECTIONS

Infections may or may not cause itching. The most well-known fungal infection is called "ringworm." The use of the word "worm" is confusing because worms have nothing to do with this disease. Yeast infections affecting the skin are diagnosed more and more frequently. Fortunately, it is a relatively straightforward process to diagnose and treat most superficial bacterial infections and abscesses due to cat bites.

The challenging cases are those that have a coexisting complicating disease, extend deeper into the skin and subcutaneous tissue, or seem to be constantly recurring. The emotions and frustrations felt by pet owners in these situations are similar to those parents may feel when their child suffers from chronic or recurrent ear infections.

Various problems may predispose a cat to unusual or recurring infections. Feline leukemia virus and feline immunodeficiency virus can alter the immune system and should always be considered as a potential factor—even in patients who have been vaccinated. Drugs such as steroids and anti-cancer therapy can have similar actions. Diseases such as diabetes and liver problems can also be associated with an altered immune response and subsequent infections.

Microscopic examination of samples taken from the skin may be necessary to confirm a suspected infection and occasionally, cultures or skin biopsies may be necessary as well. In some situations, your veterinarian may elect to refer you and your pet to a board-certified veterinary dermatologist for another opinion and treatment recommendations.

In the case of complex skin diseases, your veterinarian or veterinary dermatologist may recommend reevaluating your pet during or after the use of drug therapy to ensure that the original problem has been brought under control and to see what the remaining condition looks like without secondary infections complicating the overall symptoms. In order to make sure that an infection has totally cleared, repeat examinations and tests may be necessary. Sometimes the symptoms may appear to have totally improved but the

disease is still present to a lesser extent. Longer term therapy may be needed. It can be difficult to determine if the problem is still present or if something else is contributing to the symptoms.

Sharing a home with a pet suffering from a recurring skin problem can be psychologically and financially challenging, especially when multiple problems are present. For your and your pet's sake, it is important to share your concerns with your veterinarian and understand that your pet may have a disease that may be incurable, yet systematically controlled and managed.

RINGWORM

Ringworm, or dermatophytosis, can be a dreaded diagnosis for many cat owners. Many, but not all, cases are mild and relatively easy to treat. The persistent cases or those associated with a cattery situation or a

This unfortunate black cat has acquired the fungal ailment known as ringworm.

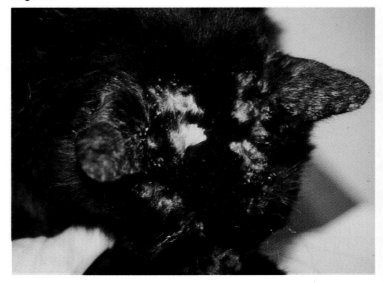

multi-cat household can be a serious challenge. Management of the condition is complicated by the fact that many cats may carry the organism that causes ringworm on their body but do not show any symptoms.

There are three main types of fungus that cause ringworm. Some types show a preference to cats over humans; some, instead, infect humans or rodents instead. However, most types can potentially affect most animal species. *Microsporum canis* is the most commonly diagnosed dermatophyte in cats and dogs. Symptoms of a ringworm infection are quite variable. The classic signs include circular areas of hair loss that initially may be red and scaly at the center. They may increase in size and progress to a darkened center with a red border. Other diseases may have a similar appearance and further testing is needed to confirm the diagnosis. Sometimes only a single area of skin is affected with the fungus, but often times multiple areas are affected at the same time. In severe cases, the whole body may be involved. Occasionally, only a nail or toe may be affected.

Other manifestations of a ringworm infection include miliary dermatitis and kerion formation. A kerion may appear similar to a "boil" or abscess. Infections from other organisms may also have a similar appearance. A cat that has a lesion with oozing discharge should be considered potentially contagious to humans and handled with care. Most of these lesions are abscesses

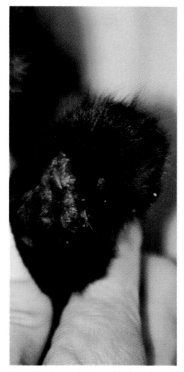

Both the top of the cat's head and his legs are affected with ringworm, which is actually a fungus and does not involve worms at all.

from cats biting each other and are not considered contagious. However, a small number of them are due to organisms that can cause a serious disease in cats as well as humans.

Diagnosis of a ringworm infection is best made by obtaining a fungal culture. This culture is performed by collecting hairs from the cat and placing them on a special culture medium. The fungi that cause ringworm produce a color change in the culture media as they grow. The most important part of the culture is the microscopic examination of the growing fungus to confirm that it is a true ringworm. Many organisms may turn the culture plate a different color

at different times while they grow, and the microscopic identification helps prevent a falsely positive diagnosis.

False positive and false negative diagnoses are perhaps even more common with the use of a Wood's lamp. A Wood's lamp is similar to a "black light." Some, but not all, ringworm organisms will be associated with an apple-green florescent glow affecting the hair shafts. Other skin diseases will also occasionally cause part of the skin or scab to glow, but usually a different color and not the hair shaft.

Sometimes, microscopic evaluation of the hair itself reveals the presence of a suspicious organism, but special chemicals are needed to dissolve the hair and a negative test result does not mean that ringworm is not present.

In summary, if these other tests are correctly interpreted and found to be positive, they can lead to the diagnosis of ringworm. However, proper treatment of ringworm can be tedious, sometimes frustrating, and is not without potential side effects. Due to the inaccuracies associated with some of the tests for ringworm and the possible side effects of treatment, a fungal culture with microscopic examination should be used to confirm the diagnosis of ringworm.

There are many different treatment options ranging from oral medications (pills and liquids) to topical therapy (shampoos and sponge-on dips). Some cats are able to clear themselves of an infection without any treatment. Some may only appear to clear up clinically but actually become carriers of the disease. Topical therapy may not actually cure the disease, but it likely helps to decrease the contamination of the environment. Newer topical therapies with greater efficacy will likely be available in the future. Oral therapy primarily consists of the use of griseofulvin, ketoconazole, and itraconazole.

Griseofulvin is the most commonly used drug and is seldom associated with side effects. Occasionally, severe side effects may be seen and thus regular monitoring is necessary. Cats with feline immunodeficiency virus appear to be more likely to have life-threatening reactions. As with many diseases, the clinical signs may improve quickly with treatment, but the disease-causing organism may remain and flare up if the treatment is discontinued too quickly. Regular reevaluations and follow-up fungal cultures are a critical part of therapy.

Ringworm can be transmitted to other pets and people. Children, the elderly, and people with an immunodeficiency are more susceptible to this disease, but anyone can catch it. The organism may even be transmitted by inanimate objects such as bedding materials, towels, or brushes. Thsse items can be replaced, and should be replaced, during the course of treatment at least once. However, washing with hot water and dilute bleach is satisfactory in some cases.

Washing all surfaces that can be washed (floors, countertops, cages, shelves,

Once a diagnosis of ringworm has been made, the cat's entire environment must be thoroughly washed, as this disease can be transmitted to other pets, as well as humans, in the household.

etc.) is also necessary. Carpeting is a special challenge and should be handled on an individual basis. Daily vacuuming is advisable. Steam cleaning probably does not produce temperatures high enough to kill the organism but should

help further clean this difficult-to-clean surface.

Vaccination for ringworm has received a great deal of publicity. However, the product literature claims are based upon clinical signs and Wood's lamp findings. As discussed, the sole use of

The fluorescent nature of this photo is the result of a Woods lamp examination, one method of identifying ringworm.

these criteria would potentially miss many cases of ringworm. Cats who carry the disease without showing symptoms can be frustrating to both the pet owner and the veterinarian. The situation complicates the diagnosis and management of this disease. Scientific studies involving ringworm cultures as a measure of success in achieving a cure or prevention of the disease are necessary to ensure true efficacy. Few veterinary dermatologists recommend the use of this vaccine.

Other types of infection such as sporotrichosis, nocardia, plague, and leprosy are occasionally a problem. Coexisting diseases that affect the cat's immune status may be present. Sporotrichosis is a disease caused by a fungus and can be transmitted to humans. In cats, the disease is usually progressive and life threatening. With most of these diseases, confirming the diagnosis can sometimes be as much of a challenge as the treatment.

HAIR LOSS AND HORMONAL DISEASES:

Hair loss can occur with both hormonal and non-hormonal diseases. If your pet is not causing the hair loss by chewing, itching, licking, or rubbing, and does not have an infection, then a hormonal disease may be the reason. Other causes include an unbalanced diet, stress, genetic diseases, and, in rare cases, skin cancer.

Most hormonal diseases are not typically associated with significant itching unless they have predisposed a patient to an

infection, which in turn has caused itching. However, sometimes the combination of dry skin and a dry environment can cause a pet with a hormonal disease to exhibit itching. Your veterinarian or veterinary

dermatologist may rely on a combination of clinical signs, history, special blood tests, skin biopsies and possibly other tests to determine which disease(s) may be present.

Thoroughly wash your hands after treating a cat with infectious disease, as many a caring owner has been afflicted with contagious skin disease, along with their pet.

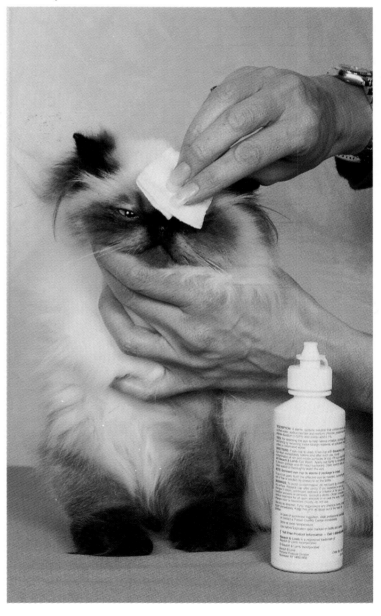

A brand new, healthy cat can emerge after being properly diagnosed and treated by a veterinarian or veterinary specialist.

STEROID-RELATED DISEASE

There are different types of steroids. The diseases associated with steroids can be due to either too much or a lack of steroids. An excess (or too high a level) of corticosteroids (called Cushing's disease or hyperadrenocorticism) is the most common steroid-associated disease. The term "hyper" means excess and should not be confused with the term "hypo," which means deficiency.

The disease may be caused by an abnormality within the body itself and is then called endogenous, meaning originating from within the body. If the disease is the result of the administration of steroids by injections, by mouth, or even in very rare cases by application to the skin or ears, it is referred to as being iatrogenic, meaning "being the result of a certain treatment." Prudent and limited use of corticosteroids rarely causes problems and can be very useful in treating many skin diseases. Unfortunately, it is not uncommon for some diseases to lead to an overuse of this group of drugs.

Endogenous hyperadrenocorticism may be caused by a problem within glands of the body that produce steroids. The glands are called the adrenal glands and are located near each kidney. The disease may also be due a problem with the part of the brain that controls the adrenal glands. Various blood tests, urine tests, X-rays, and ultrasound examinations may be necessary to find out if the disease is present. The

Above: **This cat suffers from pemphigus, which is an immune-compromising disease.**

Above: **Part of the syndrome associated with pemphigus is the appearance of sores throughout the body.**

Below: **Common symptomatology is apparent in many skin disorders, which only emphasizes the need for an accurate diagnosis.**

preliminary tests are usually screening tests that are used to determine if the disease is present. Additional tests may be performed to differentiate which type of hyperadrenocorticism is present. They may be necessary to help decide which type of treatment is best.

The symptoms of excess steroids in the body are quite varied and are similar to the side effects of steroids. Sometimes they may come on so slowly that they are confused with the normal aging process.

The treatment of iatrogenic Cushing's disease involves slowly decreasing the use of steroids administered to the pet. In most cases, it is important to slowly decrease the dose of steroids to give the body a chance to adjust, and to start producing its own appropriate levels of this necessary hormone. The levels that the body produces are much less than the levels usually seen when steroids are being used to treat a disease. Decreasing steroid use may require that the underlying reason for the original use of steroid be further investigated. If this is not possible or practical, the use of other drugs to control the original symptoms may be necessary.

The treatment of endogenous Cushing's disease is quite complicated, and there are several options that your veterinarian, veterinary dermatologist, or veterinary internist may discuss with you. Cushing's disease itself can be life threatening, but so can the treatment.

The opposite of having too high a level of steroids in the body is having too little. Most cases of this involve mineralocorticoids rather that glucocorticoids. It is considered a rare disease. This disease can be life threatening and quite varied in symptoms. However, it is important not to use this diagnosis as a "scapegoat" for a pet suffering from a variety of vague symptoms. Skin-related symptoms are actually seldom noted. Just because a patient improves with prednisone therapy does not mean that the patient has a disease due to a lack of steroids being produced by the body.

HYPOTHYROIDISM

This is an extremely rare disease that refers to insufficient thyroid hormone circulating in the body. Like steroid deficiency, the diagnosis should not be made without careful testing. Some cases of hair loss that are actually self-induced by licking may respond to thyroid replacement therapy.

However, this does not mean the patient is hypothyroid.

IMMUNE-MEDIATED, OR AUTOIMMUNE, DISEASES

This group of diseases is among the most heartbreaking, due to the often severe symptoms affecting the skin and, in other parts of the body. Perhaps the most well-known disease is "lupus," which also occurs in people.

Symptoms are not always noted in the skin, but sometimes the symptoms are found only in the skin. Pemphigus is actually the most common immune-mediated disease affecting the skin of cats and usually only affects the skin. However, affected animals may act systematically ill.

Skin-related symptoms may include sores and scabs. The feet, mouth, nose, and the areas around the eyes and genitals are often the first to be affected. In severe cases, it may appear that part of the skin or foot pads has sloughed off. Patients may or may not become systematically ill.

The actual cause of this group of diseases is not known. Genetics, drugs, hormones, sun exposure, and other factors seem to play a role in some cases. The basic biology involves the effects of the body's own immune system acting against the skin or such other body organs as the kidneys or blood.

Diagnosis may involve several tests. It is important to make sure that other more common diseases are not present. These other diseases may look similar to an immune-mediated disease or be present at the same time. They can complicate the diagnosis and treatment. Bloodwork and relatively non-invasive procedures may be the first tests performed before a skin biopsy is pursued. A blood test may also be necessary before initiating some forms of treatment because of the potential side effects of treatment.

When a biopsy is performed, we are only getting a picture of what is happening at that moment in

This cat's diagnosis of infection with Norcardia was confirmed with specialized testing. The sore on his leg is also a result of this infection.

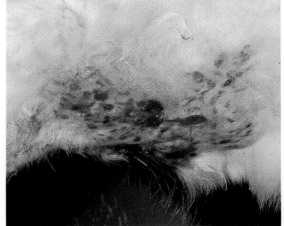

Be sure to follow your vet's instructions in treating your cat. Gentle handling—and a commitment to follow the prescribed protocol—will give your cat the best chance of restoring his health.

(a)This cat suffers from lymphoma, a condition that can cause extreme itchiness in cats. (b)Certain skin conditions can cause the skin to become thinner, and acquire a tendency to tear easily. Modification of your cat's activities may be indicated. (c)Your veterinarian will inform you as to the potential benefits, as well as risks, in any new medicinal regime.

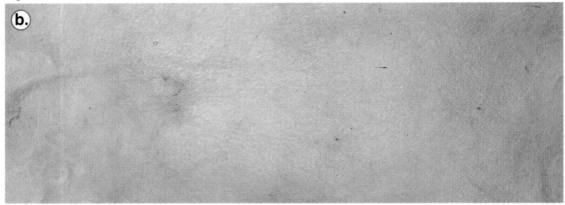

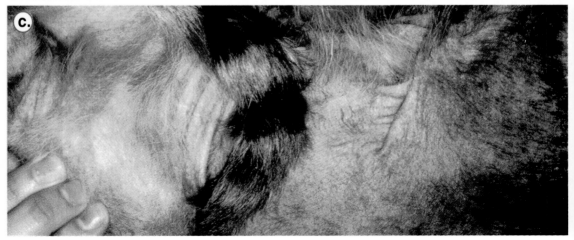

time, in that small section of skin. Site selection is very important when determining which specific location to biopsy. The biopsy should be read by a veterinary dermatologist with a special interest in skin biopsies, or a veterinary pathologist with a special interest in dermatological diseases. Even with meticulous care, an absolute diagnosis is not always possible and repeat biopsies may be necessary.

If the diagnosis of an immune-mediated disease is made, then high doses of steroids or other drugs to suppress the immune system may be used to control the symptoms. Because of the life-threatening nature of immune-mediated diseases and the potential side effects associated with their treatment, follow-up tests and regular reevaluations by your veterinarian or veterinary dermatologist are often necessary.

SEBORRHEA (EXCESSIVELY FLAKY OR OILY SKIN OR HAIR COAT)

This "disease" is really a symptom in most cases and may be caused by a variety of conditions. When seborrhea is caused by another disease, the term "secondary seborrhea" is used. Most of these causes are discussed elsewhere in this book. If an underlying cause cannot be determined, the term "primary seborrhea" or "idiopathic seborrhea" is used.

If your pet has seborrhea, it is important to find an underlying reason because treatment for idiopathic seborrhea can be quite

unrewarding. Allergies, hormonal imbalances, parasites, infections, skin cancer, and other diseases should be considered. The term primary seborrhea is used if tests for underlying diseases do not indicate an underlying cause for the symptoms and a skin biopsy is compatible with the diagnosis of primary seborrhea. Your veterinarian or veterinary dermatologist will likely try to make sure that that no other diseases are present to complicate the symptoms before selecting a location to biopsy.

The clinical signs of seborrhea vary greatly among individuals. Symptoms ranging from dry flakes to

excessive oiliness or greasiness are common. The situation can be quite confusing because infections can make a pet look and smell as if primary seborrhea is present, and, patients with primary seborrhea are prone to secondary infections.

If an underlying reason for the symptoms cannot be determined, lifelong therapy will likely be necessary. Treatment options usually center around controlling the secondary infections and shampoo therapy. However, the "high maintenance" nature of the methods used to control the symptoms and its variable sucess can lead to a poor quality of life for all members of the household.

As your cat ages, his nutritional needs change. To maintain optimum health, it's important to feed a diet with the highest quality ingredients designed for his age and condition. Photo courtesy of Nature's Recipe Pet Foods.

A modification in diet can be quite beneficial in the treatment of food allergies. However, the diet must be strictly adhered to in order to rule out any other factors contributing to your cat's intolerance.

MEDICATIONS AND SUPPLEMENTS

Medications are an important part of helping to treat a pet's skin problems. Both topical therapy (shampoos, sprays, lotions, and creams) and systemic therapy (medications given orally or by injection) are often utilized. Some topical medications are so strong that they can have systemic actions and side effects. The following section will discuss systemic medications such as steroids, antihistamines, fatty acids, antibiotics, hormonal therapy, and ivermectin.

STEROIDS

Perhaps the most useful and potentially abused systemic medication used to treat certain skin disorders is the group of drugs known as steroids. The type of steroid used to treat skin problems in animals is different than the type of steroid most people think of in association with human body builders. Anabolic steroids are used by humans to increase lean muscle mass and are associated with many potential side effects. They are classified as a "controlled substance." Glucocorticoids (corticosteroids) are in a different class of steroids and are used in animals as well as humans to control inflammation, itching, and to suppress the immune system. They have many actions and are useful in a variety of diseases. Unfortunately, they also have numerous potential

side effects.

Steroids are the most well-known drug used to control itching and are an important part of the treatment of immune-mediated diseases such as pemphigus and lupus. They may also go by names such as cortisone, prednisone, methylprednisone (Medrol), and triamcinolone (Vetalog) and may be administered in pill form or by injection. This group of drugs is effective in controlling many of the

causes of itching in dogs but has significant long-term and not-always-obvious side effects. Potential short-term side effects include altered behavior, increased water consumption, increased urination, increased appetite, panting, and pancreatitis, which may be life threatening. Long-term side effects are many and varied.

Basically, the steroids we give act to inhibit the body from producing its own steroids. This upsets the

A specially manufactured toothbrush is available on the market just for owners who want to keep their cats' teeth pearly-white. Or, you can use it to comb whiskers!

normal hormonal balance. Other side effects include diabetes, weight gain, behavior changes, liver damage, poor hair coat, demodectic mange, thin skin, comedones (blackheads), and hair loss. The body's defenses are compromised and infections may result. The symptoms may make a cat appear as if premature aging is occurring.

Some patients' diseases may appear to become resistant to steroids after long-term use. Often, this is because of a secondary infection or the occurrence of another disease. Once the infection or other disease has been controlled, the symptoms may once again be responsive to the same steroid. However, sometimes it may be necessary to change the type of steroid being used to treat a particular disease. Obviously, if these problems have been noted, the use of steroids should be reduced or eliminated.

To decrease potential side effects with long-term use, daily administration of steroids should be avoided. However, cats are more tolerant and resistant to steroids than dogs, and side effects are less common. Some diseases are so severe that daily use of steroids is necessary. In most cases, prednisone (prednisolone or methylprednisolone) should not be given more frequently than once every forty-eight hours for long-term use. Triamcinolone (Vetalog) remains in the body slightly longer than prednisone and should not be given more frequently than every three days if chronic use is

required. Use the days without medication to give the body a chance to recover and return to normal. For this reason, long-term steroid injections (such as Depo Medrol or betamethasone) that help reduce symptoms for several weeks should be avoided if possible. Symptoms may actually return before the injectable steroid has entirely worked its way out of the system. Doses of steroids that cause severe problems in a dog may be well-tolerated in a cat. Long-term injections can even be well tolerated in some cases.

Perhaps the most dramatic side effect seen with steroid use is easily tearing or ripping skin. This frightening problem typically occurs during routine handling and can be extensive. The tears do not typically bleed significantly because the skin and blood vessels have become thin and small. Placement of stitches can be difficult because the skin may tear as the stitches are used to pull the skin together.

Long-term and severe side effects are more likely with injections than pills. Another advantage of the pill formulation is that if your pet gets sick and should not be given any more steroids, most pill formulations will be out of the pet's system after a day or two. Once a long-term injection of a steroid is administered, the drug remains in the body for a long time and cannot be removed.

Steroids provide a very important form of therapy. If used wisely, they are generally safe. Short-term use seldom causes serious problems. If steroids are

needed for months or years, other options should be considered. As always, it is best to have a diagnosis and identify an underlying reason for the symptoms before using steroids. This is especially important when long-term use of these drugs is necessary. For this reason, many pet owners may be referred to a board-certified veterinary dermatologist.

Severe, life-threatening diseases may require very high doses of steroids, and your veterinarian or veterinary dermatologist may consider using other drugs that suppress the immune system. These other drugs may include chlorambucil (Leukeran), gold therapy, or other drugs. The drugs are associated with various side effects that can sometimes lead to a life-threatening situation, such as a drop in the number of white blood cells. They may be used in conjunction with steroids to help lower the dose of each type of drug necessary to control the symptoms.

OTHER DRUGS (ANTIHISTA-MINES AND FATTY ACIDS) USED TO CONTROL ITCHING AND ITS INFLAMMATION

In addition to steroids, there are other drugs that can be utilized to decrease the inflammation associated with itching. These options include antihistamines and fatty acids. In order to understand how medical therapy is effective, it helps to think of three separate and individual pathways that lead to inflammation and itching. Steroids block all three pathways, but because of their side effects, drugs that help block the individual pathways should be considered.

Antihistamines include drugs such as hydroxyzine, diphenhydramine, and chlorpheniramine. They help block only one of the three main pathways that lead to inflammation and itching. Antihistamines work better as a preventative, but they can be used on an "as-needed" basis if the itching has not become severe. Although generally safe, this group of drugs can have side effects such as sedation, excitation, and an increased risk of seizures in pets with such a predisposition. They should not be used without consulting a veterinarian.

Drugs with psychological actions can also be helpful in controlling itch. Amitriptyline (Elevil), a drug used as an antidepressant in humans, has rather potent antihistaminic actions in dogs and can be as beneficial as antihistamines in treating allergy-induced itching in many pets. Diazepam (Valium) has also been shown to be beneficial in some situations but has occasionally been associated with a fatal liver problem.

Fatty acids are available in powder, liquid, and capsule formulations. They help block another of the individual pathways that lead to inflammation but may require six to eight weeks of use until maximum effect may be observed. Fatty acids work better as a preventative measure rather than stopping the inflammation once it has become a problem. They also help control dry or flaky skin, which can also cause itching.

A great deal of thoughtful consideration has been ascribed to the medical specialty known as veterinary dermatology, and inroads continue to be made in this exciting specialty.

There are many different brand names of this type of drug. The optimum ratio of specific ingredients has yet to be determined. Label claims of greater quantity of important ingredients do not necessarily correlate with a greater success rate. The use of formulations that have undergone clinical trials proving their efficacy is recommended.

The use of drugs other than steroids to control itching is less convenient but reduces the potential for serious side effects. If these other drugs are not totally effective in controlling clinical signs, they often help reduce the amount of steroids that are necessary to decrease itching. The costs of antihistamines and fatty acids are usually greater than the costs of steroids. However, the costs of side effects and diseases associated with excessive steroid use can be substantial in both monetary and health-related terms.

For patients with allergic inhalant dermatitis, the use of immunotherapy injections based on intradermal skin testing may provide a cost-effective alternative. Some patients require a combination of various treatments in order to maintain an adequate comfort level without incurring side effects due to overuse of one drug. The importance of identifying the underlying and coexisting cause(s) of itching cannot be overemphasized. It is also important to note that the original cause of the symptom may be different from the cause of the reappearance of the symptom. For instance, itching may originally be due

to allergies. A reappearance of itching may be due to fleas or mites.

ANTIBIOTICS AND ANTIMICROBIAL DRUGS

Bacterial and yeast infections are problems associated with many different types of skin diseases. While they may not be the pet's primary problem, identifying and treating these infections is a very important component in improving the patient's condition. It is important to make sure that these medications are given as directed and for the full amount of time prescribed. In complex skin diseases, your veterinarian or veterinary dermatologist may recommend reevaluating your pet after the use of these drugs to ensure that the infections have been brought under control, and to see what the remaining condition looks like without secondary infections complicating the overall symptoms.

There are many different types of antibiotics. When utilized to treat bacterial skin infections, they are usually used for a minimum duration of three weeks. Perhaps the most common side effect is an upset stomach or diarrhea, and this can be seen with various types of antibiotics. Other adverse reactions are also possible, but fortunately life-threatening side effects are very uncommon. Bacteria may become resistant to a certain type of antibiotic, which may require that the antibiotic be changed. With long-term or repeated use, they may predispose a

patient to a yeast infection. This is one example of why a reevaluation may be necessary. The recurrence of symptoms may be due to either a yeast infection or a return of the bacterial infection.

Yeast infections may occur in the ear as well as on the skin. There is often an underlying disease present, and the infections can be a recurring problem. Some yeast infections can be controlled with topical therapy, while others require systemic medications. Topical medications range from a vinegar-and-water-mixture to prescription preparations. Prescription medications administered by mouth (such as ketoconazole) can be quite

helpful but are often expensive and can be associated with side effects. For these reasons, ketoconazole is seldom prescribed or refilled without confirmation of the diagnosis of yeast through the use of a microscopic examination.

Griseofulvin is the most commonly prescribed oral medication to treat ringworm.

HORMONAL THERAPY

Besides steroids, the most common hormone used in cats is megestrol acetate (Ovabana). It is a progesterone-like drug, and its actions and uses are similar to steroids. However, more severe side effects are often seen. Diabetes, infections of the uterus, and mammary gland tumors are

Like all other animals, cats love special food treats. When you go to the trouble and time to maximize your cat's health by feeding a diet with the highest quality ingredients, don't skimp on treats or you could have a problem anyway. Photo courtesy of Nature's Recipe Pet Foods.

not uncommon. For these reasons, the use of this drug should be avoided.

IVERMECTIN

Ivermectin has revolutionized the treatment for many types of feline parasites. However, because the drug is not approved for use in cats in the US, it is important to be aware of its indications and potential side effects.

Ivermectin belongs to a class of chemicals called the *avermectins*. This class appears to be one of the most potent broad-spectrum antiparasitic agents known. In nature, ivermectin is produced by an organism in the soil. In cats, side effects are extremely rare, but death has been reported.

Extralabel use of ivermectin has been shown to be effective in the treatment of ear mites *(Otodectes cynotis)*, scabies *(Notoedres cati)*, and cheyletielosis *(Cheyletiella blakei)*. The efficacy of ivermectin in the treatment of feline demodicosis remains undetermined. It has shown promise in the treatment of canine demodicosis. In short, ivermectin is a powerful tool in the treatment of many feline parasites.

VITAMINS AND MINERALS

Our understanding of cats' dietary needs has improved in recent years. Cats fed a well-balanced and complete diet seldom benefit from additional vitamin supplements. Indiscriminate supplementation can have potentially harmful effects, especially with non-water-soluble vitamins. However, many veterinarians and

veterinary dermatologists recommend moderate doses of vitamin E as an aid in the treatment of a variety of diseases ranging from demodectic mange to discoid lupus. One should be careful when supplementing with vitamins and minerals. Some of them have the potential to bind up or compete with other vitamins and minerals, and may actually do more harm than good.

YEAST, GARLIC, SEAWEED, SHARK CARTILAGE, AND OTHER SUPPLEMENTS

It seems that every time you turn around, someone is recommending a new and/or all-natural supplement. Their recommendations are usually based on personal experience or testimonials. While experiences are important, good scientific studies are necessary to prove that the beneficial effects are due to the product rather than sheer coincidence or other factors. Some of these products are based on a piece of scientific medicine, but that does not mean that the product, as a whole, is good. Fortunately, most of these supplements have minimal side effects. It is perfectly understandable to want to try some of these therapies because of the chronic and often incurable nature of many skin problems.

Without scientific studies, it is difficult to determine which products I would recommend. Admittedly, my medical training has been in the traditional sciences. I do believe that there is a great deal about many diseases that we do not know, and I feel certain that new

medications and treatments will continue to be discovered that improve the quality of life for our animal friends. The most effective therapies of the future will be based on good science and will be able to withstand the test of scrutiny by numerous researchers as well as large numbers of patients.

SUMMARY OF MEDICATIONS

The preceding discussion of various medications and supplements is by no means complete nor is it a substitute for veterinary care. With virtually all drugs, side effects are possible, and they should be discussed with your veterinarian. Life-threatening reactions are rare but can potentially occur with any drug. Even drugs that are available over the counter can have devastating side effects.

In some cases, the symptoms of a particular disease and the signs of side effects of a certain medication may be very similar. A reevaluation by a veterinarian or veterinary dermatologist may reveal the presence of a new disease, a drug-related side effect, or the recurrence of a previously controlled disease. Often follow-up examinations and tests are necessary to make sure that the original problem has totally cleared.

Sometimes the symptoms may appear to have totally improved, but the disease is still present to a much reduced degree. Longer term therapy may be needed. Without follow-up, it can be difficult to determine if the original problem is still present or if something else is contributing to the symptoms.

SUGGESTED READING

TS-250
Skin & Coat Care for
Your Cat-Lowell
Ackerman, DVM

TS-271
The Allure of the Cat
Richard H. Gebhardt
John Bannon

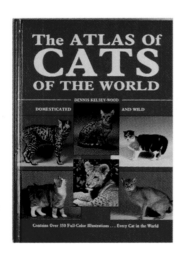

TS-127
The Atlas of Cats of The World

TW-103-The Proper
Care of Cats